SpringerBriefs in Computer Science

More information about this series at http://www.springer.com/series/10028

Flávia C. Delicato · Paulo F. Pires
Thais Batista

Resource Management for Internet of Things

 Springer

Flávia C. Delicato
Department of Computer Science
Federal University of Rio de Janeiro
Rio de Janeiro
Brazil

Paulo F. Pires
Department of Computer Science
Federal University of Rio de Janeiro
Rio de Janeiro
Brazil

Thais Batista
Department of Informatics and Applied
  Mathematics
Federal University of Rio Grande do Norte
Natal, Rio Grande do Norte
Brazil

ISSN 2191-5768   ISSN 2191-5776 (electronic)
SpringerBriefs in Computer Science
ISBN 978-3-319-54246-1   ISBN 978-3-319-54247-8 (eBook)
DOI 10.1007/978-3-319-54247-8

Library of Congress Control Number: 2017932427

Printed on acid-free paper

This Springer imprint is published by Springer Nature
The registered company is Springer International Publishing AG
The registered company address is: Gewerbestrasse 11, 6330 Cham, Switzerland

Preface

The emergent paradigm of Internet of Things (IoT) promises to take the integration of people with communications and sensing technologies to a new level. With the possibility of addressing each physical object individually and making it part of a global network, the IoT will enable new applications that can revolutionize human behaviour and interactions. The IoT has the potential to provide novel value-added services to make life easier and healthier for citizens, to increase the productivity of companies and to promote the construction of more intelligent and sustainable cities, environments and countries. Despite the great interest on IoT, there is yet to be an agreed definition of such a concept. The IoT concept is difficult to capture and shape, owing to the complex ecosystem formed not only by the variety of its constituent elements but also by the vast possibilities of interaction models that arise in such an environment. In order to effectively take advantage of the vast number of connected things, applications need to be built that exploit the data generated by IoT devices and transform them into information capable of assisting decision-making processes and ultimately into valuable knowledge for users. The wide range of software and hardware elements required for processing, analysing, transmitting, and temporarily or permanently storing the data produced by things compose an IoT ecosystem. In addition, since the ultimate goal of IoT applications is to provide services to end-users, the human being is also an integral part of this ecosystem. Their needs, social habits, desires, characteristics and context of daily activities should be considered when building a truly useful IoT system.

Despite its potential benefits, there are still many challenges to be overcome to leverage the wide dissemination of the IoT paradigm. One major challenge is efficiently managing the resources involved in an IoT ecosystem. From the acquisition of physical data to its transformation into valuable services or information, there are several steps that must be performed, involving the various players in the complex IoT ecosystem. Such transformation consists of a process that demands resources from the system. IoT devices, such as sensors, have limited computing and energy resources, and they are not able to perform sophisticated processing and storing large amounts of data. Therefore, it is often necessary to rely on more powerful devices to fully perform the transformation process required by

IoT applications. Such devices can vary from smartphones to gateway nodes to geographically distributed data centres of different scales. Indeed, with its vast capacity of processing and long-term storage, cloud computing comes hand-in-hand with IoT to create complex, large-scale, distributed and data-oriented ecosystems. Therefore, the interplay of IoT devices, gateways, cloud nodes and other elements to achieve the final goal of producing useful information to end-user gives rise to a management problem that needs to be wisely tackled.

This book focuses on the resource management problem in IoT systems from a broad perspective. The core issue of this problem is how to allocate the resources available in the heterogeneous IoT system to accommodate the requirements imposed by applications. At the first glance, this issue is similar to the typical resource allocation and task scheduling problems, which have been exhaustively studied in several areas of computing systems. However, resource allocation for IoT poses new challenges that call for novel solutions, tailored for such an emerging scenario. The huge heterogeneity of the participant devices (from tiny sensors to powerful data centre nodes), the highly dynamic execution environment, the specific nature of the data generated by IoT devices, are examples of issues that make IoT a very peculiar ecosystem. Moreover, there are several activities that, although not in the core of the problem, are required to support the resource allocation, such as resource discovery and monitoring. We believe that resource management (including allocation and scheduling decisions, but not limited to these) is a key issue to deal with the diverse nature of IoT resources and to optimize the overall system performance, thus benefiting both end-users and infrastructure/device owners. Considering the relevance of this subject and its complexity, in this book we present a thorough study of the activities encompassed in a holistic resource management process for IoT, with emphasis on resource allocation. This book does not focus on the algorithmic solutions for resource allocation, but instead on the different functionalities and architectural approaches involved on a basic workflow for managing the life cycle of resources in an IoT system.

This book should be of interest for researchers, students, professional developers who are interested in studying the IoT paradigm from the perspective of how to manage the dynamic and heterogeneous resources involved from the data acquisition to the delivering of value-added services for the end-user.

Rio de Janeiro, Brazil   Flávia C. Delicato
Rio de Janeiro, Brazil   Paulo F. Pires
Natal, Brazil   Thais Batista
January 2017

Contents

Chapter 1
Introduction

Abstract The emergent paradigm of Internet of Things (IoT) promises to take the integration of people with communications and sensing technologies to a new level. With the possibility of addressing each physical object individually and make it part of a global network, the IoT has the potential to provide novel value-added services to make life easier and healthier for citizens, to increase the productivity of companies and to promote building more intelligent and sustainable cities, environments and countries. Despite its potential benefits, there are still many challenges to be overcome to leverage the wide dissemination and adoption of the IoT paradigm. One major challenge in this context is *efficiently managing the resources involved in an IoT ecosystem*. From the acquisition of physical data to its transformation into valuable services or information, there are several steps that must be performed, involving the various players in the complex IoT ecosystem. Such transformation consists of a process that demands *resources* from the system. IoT devices, such as sensors, have limited computing and energy resources, and they are not able to perform sophisticated processing and storing large amounts of data. Therefore, it is often necessary to rely on more powerful devices to fully perform the transformation process required by IoT applications. Such devices can vary from smartphones to gateway nodes to geographically distributed data centres of different scales. Considering the relevance of this subject and its complexity, the purpose of this book is to discuss the issues regarding resource management in IoT from a holistic perspective. Our goal is investigating the core activities encompassed in a holistic resource management process for IoT, with emphasis on resource allocation. We will not focus on the algorithmic solutions for resource allocation, but instead, on the different functionalities and architectural approaches involved on a basic workflow for managing the lifecycle of resources in an IoT system.

Keywords Internet of Things (IoT) · Resource management · Resource allocation · Resource discovery · Resource modelling

F.C. Delicato et al., *Resource Management for Internet of Things*,
SpringerBriefs in Computer Science, DOI 10.1007/978-3-319-54247-8_1

1.1 Motivation

We are experiencing a moment in human history in which technological innova-
tions occur at an unprecedented pace. Technology has changed the way people live
individually and in society, and how they interact with the environment. There is no
doubt that the Internet was one of the technologies of highest impact in the last
decades, affecting the way how the information is handled and accessed, and creating new models of service provision and delivery. Of equal importance on human
life are the technological advances that enabled ubiquitous computing, encompassing from wireless communication networks to sophisticated micro-electronic
circuits that allowed building intelligent sensors and actuators. The emergent
paradigm of Internet of Things (IoT) [1, 2] promises to take the integration of
people with communications and sensing technologies to a new level. With the
possibility of addressing each physical object individually and make it part of a
global network, the IoT will enable new applications that can revolutionize human
behaviour and interactions. The IoT has the potential to provide novel value-added
services to make life easier and healthier for citizens, to increase the productivity of
companies and to promote the construction of more intelligent and sustainable
cities, environments and countries. Despite the great interest on IoT, there is yet to
be an agreed definition of such a concept. The IoT concept is difficult to capture and
shape, owing to the complex ecosystem formed not only by the variety of its
constituent elements, but also by the vast possibilities of interaction models that
arise in such an environment.

The term "Internet of Things" was first introduced by Kevin Ashton in a talk in
1998 [3]. Thereafter, the MIT Auto-ID centre, which Ashton helped create in 1999,
presented their IoT vision in 2001 [4]. This initial vision of IoT was centred in a
perspective in which the "things" consisted merely of objects identified by the joint
use of Electronic Product Code (EPC) [4] and radio-frequency identification (RFID)
tags. From the initial vision of IoT, enabled mainly by the use of RFIDs, nowadays
such concept has evolved to a broader view that refers to the interconnection of
sensors, actuators and other intelligent objects, extending the existing interactions
between man and machine provided by the current Internet to a new dimension of
man–object communication and object–objects.

Gartner [1] defines IoT as "… the network of dedicated physical objects (things)
that contain embedded technology to sense and/or interact with their internal state
or external environment". In the IoT, 'things' refer to potentially any object on the
surface of the Earth, provided that it is instrumented with sensing/actuating devices
and preferably (but not necessarily) a wireless interface. However, it is not only the
so-called smart things that compose the IoT, but instead it encompasses several
physical and virtual elements, composing a complex system (or a system of

[1]http://www.gartner.com/it-glossary/internet-of-things/.

systems [5]). To effectively take advantage of the vast number of connected things, applications need to be built that exploit the data generated by IoT devices and transform them into information capable of assisting decision-making processes and ultimately into valuable knowledge for users. The wide range of software and hardware elements required for processing, analysing, transmitting and temporarily or permanently storing the data produced by things compose an IoT ecosystem. In addition, as the ultimate goal of IoT applications is to provide services to end users, the human being is also an integral part of this ecosystem. Their needs, social habits, desires, characteristics and context of daily activities should be considered when building a truly useful IoT system.

Despite its potential benefits, there are still many challenges to be overcome to leverage the wide dissemination and adoption of the IoT paradigm. One major challenge in this context is *efficiently managing the resources involved in an IoT ecosystem.* From the acquisition of physical data to its transformation into valuable services or information, there are several steps that must be performed, involving the various players in the complex IoT ecosystem. Such transformation consists of a process that demands *resources* from the system. IoT devices such as sensors have limited computing and energy resources, and they are not able to perform sophisticated processing and storing large amounts of data. Therefore, it is often necessary to rely on more powerful devices to fully perform the transformation process required by IoT applications. Such devices can vary from smartphones to gateway nodes to geographically distributed data centres of different scales. Indeed, with its vast capacity of processing and long-term storage, cloud computing comes hand-in-hand with IoT to create complex, large-scale, distributed and data-oriented ecosystems. Therefore, the interplay of IoT devices, gateways, cloud nodes and other elements to achieve the ultimate goal of producing useful information to end user gives rise to a management problem that needs to be wisely tackled.

1.2 Goals

In this book, we investigate the resource management problem in IoT systems from a broad perspective. The core issue of this problem is *how to allocate the resources available in the heterogeneous IoT system in order to accommodate the requirements imposed by applications.* At the first glance, this issue is similar to the typical resource allocation and task scheduling problems, which have been exhaustively studied in several areas of computing systems. However, we argue that resource allocation for IoT poses new challenges that call for novel solutions, tailored for such emerging scenario. The huge heterogeneity of the participant devices (from tiny sensors to powerful data centre nodes), the highly dynamic execution environment and the specific nature of the data generated by IoT devices are examples of issues that make IoT a very peculiar ecosystem. Moreover, there are several activities that, although not in the core of the problem, are required to support the resource allocation, such as resource discovery and monitoring. We believe that resource management (including allocation and scheduling decisions, but not limited to these) is a key issue to deal with the diverse nature of IoT resources and optimize the overall system performance, thus benefiting both end users and infrastructure/device owners.

Considering the relevance of this subject and its complexity, in this book we present a thorough study of the activities encompassed in a holistic resource management process for IoT, with emphasis on resource allocation. We will not focus on the algorithmic solutions for resource allocation, but instead, on the different functionalities and architectural approaches involved on a basic workflow for managing the lifecycle of resources in an IoT system. The starting point for our study was a systematic review of the existing literature in the field. By adopting a review process based on a well-defined methodology [6, 7], we retrieved a set of studies that served as input for our discussion and analysis presented in this book. From an initial number of 586 papers retrieved in our search, and after a careful filtering process to remove poorly quality or non-relevant works, a total of 45 studies were considered useful for our discussions. From these studies, we identified the main approaches to accomplish each activity identified as necessary for the resource management in IoT. Several surveys were already published on the field of resources allocation/scheduling for cloud computing [8, 9] and wireless sensor networks (WSN) [10], two areas directly correlated to IoT. However, to the best of our knowledge, there is no existing survey in the field of IoT targeting this specific issue and with the focus we adopt in our Book. Therefore, we believe this book will provide a useful material for the reader interested in studying the IoT paradigm from the perspective of how to manage the dynamic and heterogeneous resources involved from the data acquisition to the delivering of value-added services for end users.

1.3   Overview of the Book

The remainder of the book is organized as follows. Chapter 2 presents some background concepts and our view on the resource management challenge for IoT in terms of its requirements and activities involved. Chapter 3 describes the activity of resource modelling and presents some approaches for performing such activity. Chapter 4 describes the activities of resource discovery and resource estimation, presenting some examples of existing works tackling such activities as well as their specific challenges in IoT. Chapter 5 details the activity of resource allocation, discussing existing works for performing such activity with different architectures and approaches. Chapter 6 discusses open issues and presents our concluding remarks.

References

1. Al-Fuqaha A, Guizani M, Mohammadi M, Aledhari M, Ayyash M (2015) Internet of things: a survey on enabling technologies, protocols, and applications. IEEE Commun Surv Tutorials 17(4):2347–2376
2. Atzori L, Iera A, Morabito G (2010) The Internet of Things: a survey. Comput Netw 54 (15):2787–2805. doi:10.1016/j.comnet.2010.05.010
3. Kevin A (2009) That 'Internet of Things' thing, in the real world things matter more than ideas. RFID J 22:1
4. Brock DL (2001) The electronic product code (EPC). Auto-ID Center White Paper MIT-AUTOID-WH-002
5. Nielsen CB, Larsen PG, Fitzgerald J, Woodcock J, Peleska J (2015) Systems of systems engineering: basic concepts, model-based techniques, and research directions. ACM Compu Surv (CSUR) 48(2):18
6. Keele S (2007) Guidelines for performing systematic literature reviews in software engineering. Technical report, Ver. 2.3 EBSE
7. Petersen K, Feldt R, Mujtaba S, Mattsson M (2008) Systematic mapping studies in software engineering. In: 12th international conference on evaluation and assessment in software engineering. vol 1. sn,
8. Singh S, Chana I (2016) A survey on resource scheduling in cloud computing: issues and challenges. J Grid Comput 14(2):217–264
9. Zhan Z-H, Liu X-F, Gong Y-J, Zhang J, Chung HS-H, Li Y (2015) Cloud computing resource scheduling and a survey of its evolutionary approaches. ACM Compu Surv (CSUR) 47(4):63
10. Ahmad A, Ahmad S, Rehmani MH, Hassan NU (2015) A survey on radio resource allocation in cognitive radio sensor networks. IEEE Commun Surv Tutorials 17(2):888–917

Chapter 2
The Resource Management Challenge in IoT

Abstract The purpose of this book is to discuss the issues regarding resource management in Internet of Things (IoT) from a holistic standpoint. In order to build the foundation on which our discussion will be conducted, in this chapter we first introduce some basic definitions that are relevant to our study, such as resource, resource management and IoT ecosystem. Then, we identify the main requirements and challenges related to resource management in the specific context of IoT. Finally, we describe the typical activities involved in the all-embracing resource management process according to our proposed holistic view. For all purposes, we will consider throughout this book a generic scenario of an IoT ecosystem consisting of several heterogeneous interconnected devices, whose data and services (virtual and physical resources) are used by several different applications that access such pool of resources via network. IoT devices include both resource-constrained and resource-rich devices. We consider resource-rich devices as those that have the hardware and software capability to support the TCP/IP protocol suite. Besides IoT devices, the IoT ecosystem also includes gateways, edge nodes and cloud data centres.

Keywords Internet of Things (IoT) · Resource management · Resource allocation · Resource discovery · Resource modelling

2.1 What Is a Resource in the Context of IoT Ecosystems?

Internet of Things (IoT) ecosystems are complex environments encompassing many heterogeneous components. The huge amount of data generated by sensor-instrumented objects of the real world in an IoT ecosystem will impose a great demand for processing and storage resources to be transformed into useful information or services. Some applications will be latency sensitive, while other applications will require complex processing including historical data and time series analyses. Therefore, considering the typical resource constraints of IoT nodes, it is difficult to envision a real-world, ultra-scale IoT ecosystem without

© The Author(s) 2017

F.C. Delicato et al., *Resource Management for Internet of Things*,

SpringerBriefs in Computer Science, DOI 10.1007/978-3-319-54247-8_2

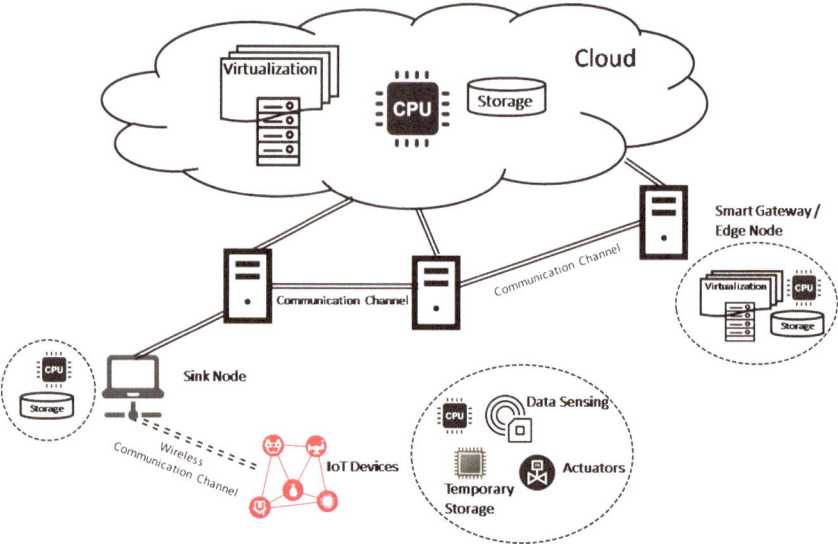

Fig. 2.1 Example of resources in an IoT ecosystem

including a cloud platform, or at least some powerful devices, for instance Smart Gateways [1] or edge/fog nodes [2]. In this complex scenario of IoT edge cloud, the definition of resource may range from physical resources, such as memory (storage), CPU, network bandwidth, energy, etc., to software resources. Procedures to perform information fusion, or to detect a complex event, or a virtualization function, are all examples of software resources. The model adopted to formally define the resource management process will depend on the definition for resource itself. So, in the same way as we are taking a holistic approach to address the resource management process, we will adopt a broad, generic and all-encompassing definition for resource:

> A resource is any object which can be allocated within a system [3].

Figure 2.1 represents an example of the resources identified in a three-tier IoT ecosystem composed of cloud, edge and IoT devices.

2.2 Key Requirements of IoT

Before starting our discussion of resource management for IoT, it is important to have a minimum understanding of the peculiarities of such environment that make it so special, requiring novel and specific solutions for such a traditional problem that has been extensively studied in computer systems. One of the goals of this book is to discuss, in depth, the specific requirements of IoT in this context, and to analyse how some existing solutions are addressing them. Therefore, we will revisit the IoT features later, at the light of the acquired knowledge on resource management. The idea of this chapter is to present a preliminary discussion to motivate for the need of new and tailored solutions.

The IoT can be seen at first glance as a sort of large-scale distributed system where the components have a high degree of **heterogeneity** with respect to hardware and software. In addition, the execution context of these systems is extremely dynamic. *Context* here has a broad meaning and it refers from the status of software components embedded in a device to the user's geographic location (which may vary in the presence of mobility) and his/her personal agenda. **Context awareness** is recognized as an important requirement of IoT systems [4] to properly accommodate the scale and heterogeneity factors and to provide useful information to meet application demands. Besides helping to build adaptive IoT systems that better fit the dynamic application needs and execution context, context awareness plays a key role in IoT to decide what data needs to be processed, based on its relevance to a given context [4].

The heterogeneity, scale and context awareness factors alone already make the resource management a very challenging issue. However, other classes of distributed systems such as clouds and ubiquitous systems share such features. We claim that the use of IoT ecosystems as infrastructure for running applications distinguishes from traditional practices in distributed systems, for the following main reasons. In dedicated distributed systems, the application software runs over infrastructures often dimensioned according to the worst case and peak scenarios. More recently, in cloud computing systems, although the service provision follows a *pay per use*, dynamic and elastic model, the application requirements are usually preestablished via formal or semiformal contracts between the client and the cloud provider. Therefore, resource allocation mechanisms in cloud platforms employ sophisticated strategies and algorithms to better allocate physical or virtual resources to applications, meeting contracts-based predefined application requirements. At runtime, such mechanisms monitor the status of the infrastructure to accommodate unforeseen demands in a scalable and elastic way, while respecting the contracts. In IoT, all the requirements of a resource allocation mechanism for cloud computing still hold, but some additional requirements emerge, as we will discuss next.

One major requirement is related to the ad hoc nature of IoT. In IoT scenarios, there can be opportunistic, ad hoc interactions among devices and users, leveraged by some specific contexts. For instance, a mobile device can make its resources available only for users that are in its neighbourhood for a given period of time. There is no sense in establishing any type of formal contract in this case. Instead, the device owner can have some type of incentive for making its resources available for other clients. It is also noticeable that in such scenarios, similarly to P2P networks, a same user can be a provider for a certain service while, at the same time, a client for services running in other devices. In this context, IoT systems do not fully adhere to the traditional contract-based client–server model assumed by several service-oriented distributed systems. Therefore, application requirements in terms of quality of service (QoS) are not always guaranteed to be met by the infrastructure. It is more likely to have a mixed model of service provision, in which parts of such requirements, for instance the ones being served by a cloud-integrated IoT platform, are regulated by informal contracts to some extent, while part of them just inherits the Internet best-effort model. The provision of these resources can be partially controlled by one or more service providers, while partially provided in an ad hoc, opportunistic fashion that is highly dependent on the current state and availability of the interconnected devices. Such feature of exploiting opportunistic interactions for the service provision in IoT makes the process of resource allocating and management more complex than in traditional cloud computing systems. Moreover, the establishment of a pricing model also becomes much more intricate for the service providers.

Another key requirement is real-time processing. IoT systems potentially handle hundreds, thousands or millions of parallel requests and several types of applications demand fast response, within a strict time interval. In IoT, multiple applications with potentially different requirements will be sharing the same resources. A time critical application will demand some level of priority in the access to the shared resources, in detriment of noncritical applications, to guarantee its requirements will be met. Moreover, the nature of data produced by IoT devices also affects its processing. Sensors generate, possibly in a continuous way, a huge amount of data, typically consisting of time series values, which are sampled over a specific time period, thus characterizing a data stream. The input rate of a data stream ranges from a few bytes per second to a few gigabits per second. Such input rate can be irregular, unpredictable and bursty in nature. The inherent nature of data streams does not allow one to easily make multiple passes over a stream while processing it (still retaining the usefulness of the data). Data stream processing often requires online solutions, in which data is processed and valuable information is acquired on the fly, without having the complete view of the data and without using past information. Real-time and online processing poses different requirements in terms of resources, in comparison to applications running on traditional cloud platforms.

Solutions for managing the resources involved in processing IoT data and delivering IoT services in a cost-effective and efficient way need to take these key requirements into account, besides further needs to be revealed during the discussion of the current literature used as basis for this book.

2.3 Key Activities for Resource Management in IoT

In order to describe the core activities of a generic framework for resource management in IoT, we consider a hypothetical model for an IoT ecosystem with either three or two tiers (Fig. 2.2), in which: (i) the *bottom tier* encompasses the things (IoT devices/nodes/smart objects), (ii) the *top tier* encompasses cloud nodes and (iii) an optional *middle tier* consists in Smart Gateways or edge nodes. Applications

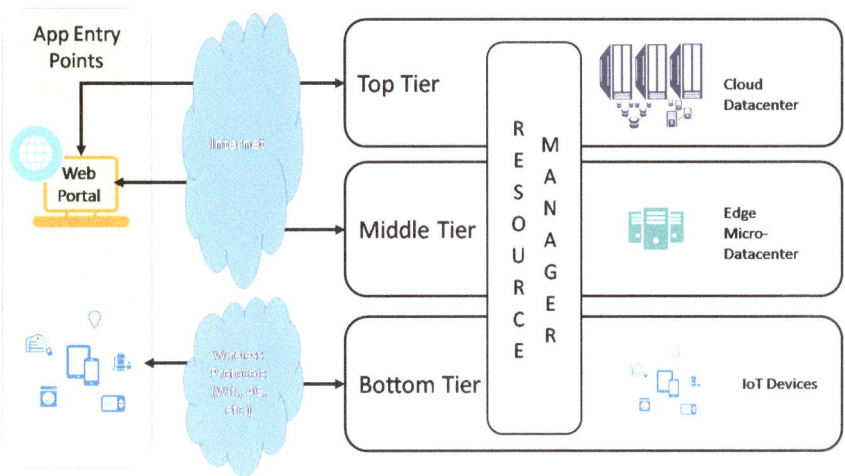

Fig. 2.2 RMS layers in IoT systems

access the system from different application entry points (AEP), sending their requests which are expected to be met by the IoT infrastructure. These entry points may themselves be physical devices which are part of the IoT bottom tier, for example, smart phones (a resource-rich IoT device), or they may be personal computers running Web portals (and thus accessing the system through the cloud) or even gateway or edge node.

Besides our hypothetical physical model organized in two or three tiers, we also assume a logical layered architecture for IoT systems. According to the authors in [5], a typical five-layer architecture for IoT encompasses: the objects layer (the lowermost in the system, representing the physical objects), the object abstraction, the service management, the application and the business layer. We claim that a resource management layer (RML) is orthogonal to the four uppermost layers proposed in [5]. The RML is responsible for all activities related to the resource management of the system. The RML will be implemented as a resource manager (RM) subsystem to be deployed in a distributed way among different hardware components in the two or three tiers of the IoT system (Fig. 2.2).

As discussed in [6], the main challenge regarding a resource management layer (RML) in the context of cloud computing is to perform the automated provisioning of resources. This is the same goal in IoT, but considering additional requirements, as aforementioned. The ultimate goal of the RML is deciding the best scheme of resource allocation according to the up-to-date system information so as to obtain the maximum utilization of the system resources. This function requires various strategies to engage the resources that meet the formally or informally established application QoS requirements. Although the resource allocation is the core of a RML, there are further activities that support such activity to enable the proper and continuous operation of the system. We identify the following activities as the main

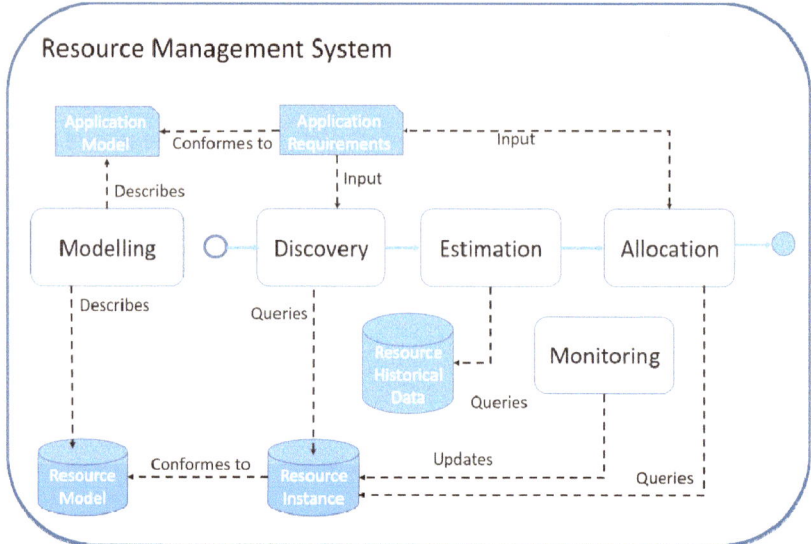

Fig. 2.3 Activities involved in the resource management

components of a typical workflow for a RMS in IoT: resource modelling, resource discovery, resource estimation, resource allocation and resource monitoring (Fig. 2.3).

The main goal of this book is to discuss all the activities encompassed in the RML, with an emphasis on the resource allocation. In the following, we briefly describe such activities, which will then be presented in the next chapters, in the light of proposals currently existing in the literature. It is important to mention that the literature search used as the starting point for the discussions presented in this book focused on works addressing resource management for IoT. The keywords used in the performed search did not explicitly include resource discovery, modelling or estimation. They are considered as support activities for the general process of resource management. Works focusing solely on such activities, without their integration in a more general framework for resource management, are not discussed in this book.

2.3.1 Resource Modelling

The first issue about the resource management process is how applications and resource management systems describe resources in an IoT ecosystem. The resource model is a vital part of any RML since it defines the entities, properties and relationships that build up the system, thus driving the whole operation of the resource manager. Moreover, using high-level models to represent resources facilitates dealing with the inherent heterogeneity of IoT resource providers. Resource models can be regarded as the scheme or metadata for describing the resources within a system. They are typically created by designers of IoT systems and are used by the resource management systems and by IoT applications for different purposes. Therefore, an important feature of modelling solutions is the ease with which (i) designers can translate IoT resources to the available modelling constructs, (ii) the applications can describe their needs in terms of the resources and (iii) the RMS can, at runtime, use and manipulate resource information for its decision-making processes.

The resource model must properly represent the elements from the different tiers of an IoT ecosystem, ranging from low-level IoT devices and hardware elements (e.g. CPU and memory) to high-level service interfaces. Moreover, not only physical, but also virtual resources need to be represented. Houidi et al. [7] advocate that virtual resources require to be described according to their properties and functionalities similarly as services are described in existing service architectures.

Each tier in an IoT system can have its own modelling requirements leading to different representation languages/formats. For instance, in order to favour interoperability, IoT devices can be represented through Web technologies such as the SSN ontology [8] for annotating sensors and sensor networks, and Linked Data [9] for sensor data publishing and discovery. Network and computing resources may be represented using existing specifications, such as Network Description Language (NDL) [10, 11].

IoT resource and services can be described with different levels of abstraction for end users/developers, and different parameters can be exposed to be tuned for optimization purposes during allocation. The granularity used to represent and expose resources is also an important issue in resource modelling [12]. For instance, a resource management system can use a particular representation model that exposes a very detailed (low-level) description of resources to the applications, giving more flexibility and allowing for a better customization of resource usage (to the applications). In this case, this flexibility comes at the cost of a harder optimization problem to be solved by the RMS. For example, if an application request is defined based on the physical specifications of each machine, the optimal matching of the request with available resources becomes harder to achieve since the possible optimization solution space is narrowed by the request itself. Finally, a resource model can be described using a formal, semiformal or informal notation. The adoption of more formal representations of resources provides more rigour to the model and allows using automatized tools for consistency checking, for verifying some properties of the model and also to exploit techniques such as reasoning, during the activity of resource discovery. Considering all these features, existing proposals for resource modelling can be analysed according to their degrees of abstraction, formalism and granularity. Other relevant characteristic are their expressivity and flexibility.

Once the resource model is built according to the selected notation, the IoT infrastructure can expose the (physical or virtual) resources for the consumer applications. IoT applications are built upon such resources, and are ultimately the triggers for the resource consumption. Applications can be specified by using a programmatic or declarative API, or using some high-level domain-specific language (DSL). Therefore, besides the **resource model**, the RML also needs to encompass a proper **application model**, which is closely related to the former. A mapping process should usually take place to translate application requirements to definitions and commands understandable by the entities that will execute the requested services (thus consuming resources). Depending on the adopted notation, the process of translating the application requests to a machine-readable specification will be more or less complex. Independently on the adopted approach, after a mapping process, an application will typically contain (i) a *set of descriptive functional requirements*, such as, for instance, the geographical location of interest, type of sensing data (along with optional information on data rate and/or time interval of interest), events to be detected or monitored, actions to be executed upon occurrence of events and (ii) an *optional set of nonfunctional (or QoS) attributes*, such as data accuracy, maximum end-to-end delay, data freshness and maximum monetary cost to be paid for the usage of the IoT infrastructure. Regarding the QoS attributes, applications usually require that the data produced by IoT devices are transmitted or processed according to some constraints, which can be strict in case of critical scenarios (for instance, time critical applications). Therefore, for some classes of applications, QoS requirements are very important and there may be a need of using some SLA enforcement to assure their meeting. On the other hand, some IoT applications are built upon opportunistic, ad hoc interactions, which preclude any formal agreements and the service is provided on a basis of a best-effort model.

Existing proposals addressing the resource modelling activity are presented and discussed in Chap. 3.

2.3.2 Resource Allocation

The processing of an application will incur in a workload for the IoT system and will produce one or more outputs. Such workload can be interpreted as the amount of resources needed to accomplish the specific tasks required by the application (e.g. sense, process and transmit 50 temperature samples, or acquire process and transmit one JPEG image, etc.). The workload may encompass the memory (e.g. bytes) and processing load (e.g. MIPS) consumed by the application, the use of sensing devices and of network bandwidth. The outcome of the application workload processing can be as simple as a scalar value (for instance, the current temperature of a given point in space), a detected event (presence of fire or occurrence of a temperature above a threshold) or it can be a preprocessed data stream continuously generated, to be used to feed some complex stream processing system.

The final goal of the resource allocation activity, which is the responsibility of a **resource allocation system** (RAS) within the RML, is to properly accommodate the workload of all the applications currently using the IoT system, by allocating the required (virtual or physical) resources so that expected outcomes of all the applications are provided and the QoS requirements are met. This implies identi-fying the several fine-grained execution units that compose an application that will produce the respective workload. Then, such execution units need to be distributed among the elements of the system, preferably in a fair, balanced way, so that the overall utilization of the system resources is optimized while satisfying the needs of simultaneous applications. The main inputs of such a resource allocation system are (i) the resource modelling (the schema used to describe the types of resources existing in the whole IoT system), (ii) current status of IoT resources (the resource instances along with their instantaneous utilization) and (iii) the application mod-elling, encompassing the set of functional and nonfunctional requirements.

Figure 2.4 depicts the activities involved in the resource allocation for IoT systems. The first step in a resource allocation is *planning*, in which a global view of the available resources is analysed to verify if the IoT system as a whole can accommodate the application requirements. Moreover, considering that the IoT system comprises multiple tiers (things, cloud and edge tiers), the planning includes the decision about which tiers are to be engaged in the execution. Next, the indi-vidual execution units (or tasks) need to be provided with the specific resources required for their execution. This step is basically a *task mapping* process, where a selected element (node) of the IoT system will be assigned a given task. There may be collaboration among entities of the IoT system to complete the required tasks of an application. Moreover, there are dependencies among different tasks of a same application that need to be considered. Therefore, as another step of the resource allocation process, the *temporal scheduling of computational tasks* should be determined respecting the application time constraints and the dependencies between tasks. Finally, it is necessary to *schedule the communication* among the entities participating in the execution of tasks on available communication

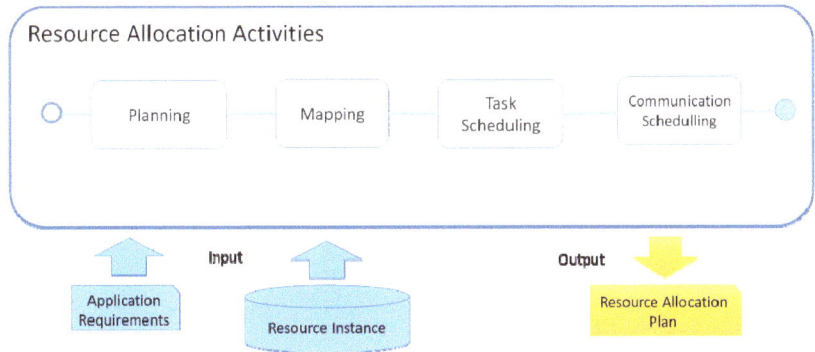

Fig. 2.4 Resource allocation activities

channels. Task mapping and scheduling must be done in an efficient and cost-effective way for both the providers and the clients (end users and applications).

Considering the dynamicity of the IoT scenario and the different requirements of several concurrent applications accessing the system, it is clear that resource allocation is not a trivial issue in IoT. It is typically considered as an optimization problem, and multiple techniques have been employed to solve it, pursuing different performance goals and meeting different constraints. It is important to mention that resources can be either provided by physical elements or by virtualized entities. When virtual entities are involved in the resource allocation, the decision about the creation/instantiation of such virtual entities is part of the typical process of resource provision in cloud systems.

This book has a special emphasis on discussing existing proposals for the resource allocation activity. Such discussion is presented in Chap. 6.

2.3.3 Resource Discovery, Monitoring and Estimation

Before the necessary resources can be allocated, they need to be discovered in the IoT ecosystem. Resource discovery in such a heterogeneous system is in itself a challenge, worsened by the current lack of standardization of protocols and formats in the field. Moreover, the high scalability of the IoT requires the RMS to provide some mechanism able to register and discover resources and services in a self-configured, efficient and dynamic way. In the traditional Internet, the DNS service discovery protocol (DNS-SD) provides a way of using standard DNS programming interfaces, servers and packet formats to browse the network for services. Although such protocol has been originally designed originally for resource-rich devices, there are some proposals for lightweight versions tailored for IoT environments, such as [13]. In Chap. 4 we discuss some works developed in the context of resource management that include service discover mechanisms.

Another activity that is necessary so that a RMS tackles the highly dynamic nature of IoT systems is resource monitoring. The execution environment is extremely dynamic, including variations related to the user, the network, the physical environment and the devices. The monitoring of these environmental variations is essential to provide a high-quality service. Moreover, the monitoring about current resource usage is also necessary for the purpose of keeping an optimum or near to optimum resource allocation. This implies that resource management for IoT should be context-aware, and the allocation process cannot be static, but rather dynamic and adaptive to accommodate such variations in the execution context. Solutions for detecting environmental changes and adapt to them will enable the delivery of enhanced context-based services, helping to provide the more cost-effective service provision and resource usage depending on the situation.

Finally, sometimes it is useful trying to estimate the amount of resources to be used to better assure the successful completion of the application. Strategies for resource estimation are usually based on keeping historical data of the consumption. Such data is obtained through the monitoring activity. In cases where there is an estimation and possibly reservation of resources, there may be eventually non-utilized resources (for instance, because there was over provisioning or because the execution conditions changed). Therefore, it may be necessary for the system to be able to reclaim such non-utilized resources, returning them to the pool of available resources. Chapter 5 discusses some proposals for resource estimation in IoT. Proposals that exploit the activity of resource monitoring with the goal of estimating resources to be consumed based on historical data (obtained through the monitoring) are also described in such Chapter. Proposals that leverage the monitoring activity to augment the efficacy of the resource allocation strategy, endowing it with context-aware adaptation features are discussed as part of the resource allocation activity in Chap. 6.

In the following chapters, we present a thorough discussion on each issue related to our holistic view of resource management in IoT, presenting the challenges involved in each activity and existing proposals to tackle them. Our discussions are grounded on the results of a painstaking review of the state of the art in this area, carried out by our research group.

References

1. Aazam M, Huh E-N (2014) Fog computing and smart gateway based communication for cloud of things. In Future Internet of Things and Cloud (FiCloud), 2014 International conference on, 2014. IEEE, pp 464–470
2. Garcia Lopez P, Montresor A, Epema D, Datta A, Higashino T, Iamnitchi A, Barcellos M, Felber P, Riviere E (2015) Edge-centric computing: vision and challenges. ACM SIGCOMM Comput Commun Rev 45(5):37–42
3. Tanenbaum AS, Woodhull AS (1992) Operating system concepts. Learning 2:3
4. Perera C, Zaslavsky A, Christen P, Georgakopoulos D (2014) Context aware computing for the internet of things: a survey. IEEE Commun Surv Tutorials 16(1):414–454. doi:10.1109/SURV.2013.042313.00197
5. Al-Fuqaha A, Guizani M, Mohammadi M, Aledhari M, Ayyash M (2015) Internet of things: a survey on enabling technologies, protocols, and applications. IEEE Commun Surv Tutorials 17(4):2347–2376
6. Zhang Q, Cheng L, Boutaba R (2010) Cloud computing: state-of-the-art and research challenges. J Internet Serv Appl 1(1):7–18
7. Houidi I, Louati W, Zeghlache D (2008) A distributed virtual network mapping algorithm. In 2008 IEEE international conference on communications. IEEE, pp 5634–5640
8. Compton M, Barnaghi P, Bermudez L, GarcíA-Castro R, Corcho O, Cox S, Graybeal J, Hauswirth M, Henson C, Herzog A (2012) The SSN ontology of the W3C semantic sensor network incubator group. Web Semant: Sci Serv Agents on the World Wide Web 17:25–32
9. Bizer C, Heath T, Berners-Lee T (2009) Linked Data-the story so far. Int J Semant Web Inf Syst 5(3):1–22
10. Beckett D, McBride B (2004) RDF/XML syntax specification (revised). W3C Recommendation 10

11. Van der Ham JJ, Dijkstra F, Travostino F, Andree HM, de Laat CT (2006) Using RDF to describe networks. Future Gener Comput Syst 22(8):862–867
12. Endo PT, de Almeida Palhares AV, Pereira NN, Goncalves GE, Sadok D, Kelner J, Melander B, Mangs J-E (2011) Resource allocation for distributed cloud: concepts and research challenges. IEEE Netw 25(4):42–46
13. Jara AJ, Martinez-Julia P, Skarmeta (2012) A Light-weight multicast DNS and DNS-SD (lmDNS-SD): IPv6-based resource and service discovery for the Web of Things. In: innovative mobile and internet services in ubiquitous computing (IMIS), 2012 sixth international conference on, 2012. IEEE, pp 731–738

Chapter 3
The Activity of Resource Modelling

Abstract In this book, we investigate the core activities encompassed in a holistic resource management process for Internet of Things (IoT), focusing on the different functionalities and architectural approaches involved on a basic workflow for managing the lifecycle of resources in an IoT system. We identified the following activities as the main components of a typical workflow for a resource management system (RMS) in IoT: resource modelling, resource discovery, resource estimation, resource allocation and resource monitoring. In this chapter, we address the first activity, namely the resource modelling. The resource model is a vital part of any RMS that aims at properly representing the elements from the different layers of an IoT ecosystem. In this chapter, we analyse existing proposals for resource modelling, focusing on solutions for both resource representation and application representation. Proposals for resource representation can be grouped into three main categories: attribute-based, semantic-based and virtualization-based. After presenting some examples for each category, we briefly discuss them under three aspects: the degrees of abstraction, granularity and formalism with which the elements are represented in the models. It is important to mention that, although several works implicitly assume some type of representation for the system resources and also for the application, in our discussion we included only the proposals that explicitly define their models, with sufficient details to shed light in the relevant aspects of such models.

Keywords Internet of Things (IoT) · Resource management · Resource modelling · Application model · Resource allocation

3.1 Resource Modelling

The studies addressing the resource modelling activity used as a seed for our discussions can be grouped into different categories, regarding their approaches and primitives used to represent resources. We identified three categories, namely *attribute-based, semantic-based* and *virtualization-based*. Each category differs

F.C. Delicato et al., *Resource Management for Internet of Things*,
SpringerBriefs in Computer Science, DOI 10.1007/978-3-319-54247-8_3

from each other regarding the degree of abstraction, granularity and formalism with which the elements are represented in the models. Following, we present examples of proposals from each group and then we briefly compare them at the light of the three aforementioned aspects.

3.1.1   Examples of Attribute-Based Approaches

The work [1] presents a straightforward approach for resource modelling in the context of shared sensor networks [2], a novel design approach for wireless sensor networks (WSN). The traditional approach for building WSNs dictates that such platforms are tailored for a single-application to meet a given efficiency metric. Considering that WSNs are the key enablers to realize the IoT vision, such fit-for-purpose, application-specific approach is neither suitable nor cost-effective. Thus, a paradigm shift is necessary to meet the ultra large-scale requirements of IoT systems. To address this challenge, the authors in [1] proposed a shared WSN approach that allows multiple applications run concurrently on different WSNs by optimizing their usage of resources according to availability and other cost metrics. Their paradigm is presented in three phases. The first phase is the resource abstraction and representation, which aims at providing a clear and rigorous representation to leverage the full potential of IoT ecosystems across WSNs and other ubiquitous resources. The proposed solution represents resources by a group of attributes, according to which functional requirement of applications would be drawn. The attributes are: (i) functional capability, (ii) levels of operation, (iii) power consumption, (iv) location, (v) duty cycling, (vi) and region of fidelity. In particular, the functional capability denotes the task(s) that a given device/ resource is able to perform. For example, if the resource is an RF unit, it has the capacity to transmit, receive data, or sense the channel (idle listening). A camera could possibly take pictures, videos at variable rates and so on [1]. The levels of operation represent details of very low level for a given operation, whose configuration may (or may not) be available for tuning in the system. For instance, a wireless radio can operate with different transmission levels (transmission powers), each level requiring different energy consumption and allowing reaching a given distance. The levels of operation are directly related with the functional capacity, since each function could have multiple levels of operation, and application requirements may indicate the specific level desired to meet the application goals. Eventually, even if a given functional capacity is available in the IoT system, the high-level requirements of the application may not be met if the desired operation level cannot be achieved. Power consumption attribute denotes a representation of the power dissipation involved in the resource usage. Location attribute refers to the geographical placement of the resource and can have different meanings and representations, ranging from a symbolic region (a given Room number, for instance) to coordinates in the global positioning system (which is currently the *de facto* when referring to location) [1]. Duty cycling represents the percentage of time a node spent turned on during its lifetime, and it reflects the temporal property of the resource, denoting its availability. Finally, the region of fidelity attribute is presented in the paper as a more relaxed definition of sensing coverage, used to denote the region in the resource's vicinity where an event can be detected/reported.

The second phase in the proposed paradigm encompasses the application representation. The authors adopt the view of an application as a finite set of functional requirements, needed over a given time duration. By knowing the available resources, and the functional requirements as dictated by the application, it is possible to reach one of two states: (1) the application requirements could be met, hence optimal assignment of tasks to resources need to take place, or (2) the current resources cannot meet the application's demands, hence new resources need to be introduced or requirements relaxed. The third phase is the mapping, which consists in assigning applications to available resources across existing WSNs. The authors adopt a linear programming (LP) formulation to solve the mapping problem. The relevant aspect of this proposal in the context of the resource modelling activity is the simple and direct approach used to represent resources, as a set of attributes. Although simple, the set of attributed defined is enough to precisely define the application requirements and to determine if the IoT system (composed of a set of shared WSNs) is able to meet such requirements.

Three other examples of proposals that adopt attributed-based resource models are [3–5]. An interesting feature of the former is the explicit inclusion of data streams as part of the resource model. The authors model *streams* as timestamped and infinite sequences of data items. Such streams represent a valuable resource in IoT systems, which are produced as outcome of some tasks (for instance, a sensing task) and consumed as input by other (processing) tasks. Therefore, it is very important that they are considered as first class entities in the resource model, although very few proposals explicitly represent streams. In the resource model presented in [4], a *task* is modelled as a directed acyclic graph (DAG) encompassing a set of operations. The edges linking such operations represent a data stream that flows from one operation to the subsequent one. In their model, to accommodate the continuous nature of data streams, they describe the resources required by each operation along time. Instead of using a static value for the required resources, or to adopt rounds/cycles during which the status of the system in terms of resources is computed, the continuous consumption of resources is modelled as continuous functions over time. The model includes functions expressing the requirements in terms of memory, disk space (in bytes) and the number of instructions per second (ips) of each operation between the deployment of the task graph and a given time t. Two other functions model the energy consumption with computation and with communication, both considering the real throughput of the output streams. In addition, the model allows expressing a set of *constraints* to specify the operation requirements regarding the execution environment, for instance, geographic location, specific type of hardware, software or sensing devices, sample rate, accuracy, response time and other QoS constraints as communication reliability, computation time and security.

The interesting feature of the resource model in the second proposal [4] is that, instead of representing resources provided to/consumed by a given device, the authors model the resources associated with each interface of a device (for example CPU cycles, data rate, buffer size). This feature allows a finer granularity in the resource allocation strategy and promotes a better sharing of the device capabilities among multiple applications. Finally, an interesting aspect of the models proposed in [5] regards the inclusion of temporary resources, offered by mobile devices entering and leaving the coverage area of a WSN, in the proposed abstraction for resources. The authors adopt an attribute-based approach for both application and resource models. They include the ephemeral resources, only available at specific places and times, as part of the system resources pool to be shared and allocated.

3.1.2 Examples of Semantic-Based Approaches

Undoubtedly, adopting a clear and rigorous representation, such as the one present in [6] is a key requirement for resource modelling. However, the high degree of heterogeneity and autonomy present in the different levels of the IoT ecosystem calls for more sophisticated mechanisms to provide interoperability among the entities of such an ecosystem. For some authors, the most challenging problem to address in IoT is heterogeneity, which is expected to exist on an unprecedented scope [7]. Different approaches have been investigated by the researchers to build interoperable IoT ecosystems [8]. A natural choice to promote interoperability at the level of resource description is applying semantic technologies. Semantic-based IoT resource modelling promotes interoperability among IoT resources, resource providers and applications and facilitates effective resource discovery, semantic reasoning and knowledge extraction [9]. Semantic-based representation of resources can be augmented by service-oriented computing to provide a homogeneous and scalable interface to model and access IoT resources. This type of resource representation creates a model where resources are consumed as a service, similarly to what happens in the Infrastructure as a Service (IaaS) and Platform as a Service (PaaS) cloud models [6, 10].

OpenIoT [11] is an example of semantic-based IoT resource management infrastructure. OpenIoT is an open source platform for IoT that provides a flexible architecture based on cloud aiming at managing the whole lifecycle of IoT applications and services. The architecture of OpenIoT includes, among other components, modules that manage the acquisition of data from sensors (X-GSN), the provision and query of semantic information (LSM), and frontend tools to the discovery and analysis of data (e.g. Definition Request and Request Presentation). The X-GSN module manages the registration, data acquisition and deployment of sensors and interconnected objects, through semantic annotation of both sensor data and metadata. The semantic annotation is done using the OpenIoT ontology that enhances existing vocabularies for IoT devices, which they call Internet Connected Objects (ICOs), including concepts that are relevant to describe a cloud-based IoT system (such as terms to annotate units of measurement and geo-location of sensors). The OpenIoT ontology is based on the W3C SSN ontology, which supports the description of sensors in terms of capabilities, measurement processes, observations and deployments [12]. The concept of *virtual sensor* is central to the OpenIoT ontology and defines anything that can compute the value of a phenomenon. Therefore, a virtual sensor can be a physical device, a computational process or both. A virtual sensor can also be an aggregation or computation over other virtual sensors, or even represent a mathematical model of a sensing environment. The representation of a virtual sensor in the ontology glues together the phenomena (what is measured), the device and its functions and processing. The data of virtual sensors is made available to other modules of the infrastructure by registering to the LSM. Such a registering is done by the X-GSN that generates the semantic annotations in RDF, according to the OpenIoT ontology, and registers them to the LSM cloud store repository. The RDF triple stored within the LSM can be queried through a Linked Data query processor that supports the SPARQL 1.1 standard. LSM provides a wide range of APIs for accessing sensor readings such as database connections and middleware APIs, which output the data following the OpenIoT ontology. The semantic annotated virtual sensors are used by the global scheduler of OpenIoT to fulfil the IoT service requests of users. IoT services are abstractions, persisted to the cloud as SPARQL service descriptions, which encompass a set of virtual sensors that are needed for delivering the service output.

The paper [13] also proposes a semantic-based approach for resource allocation of IoT services via semantic queries. The proposed framework is structured into a three-tier architecture, including the process engine layer, the semantic access layer (SAL) and the IoT services layer. Sensors and actuators capabilities are accessed and provided via IoT services. The main abstraction used to access such services is a query. When a semantic process is executed by the process engine, a SPARQL query is sent by the process engine to the SAL via a REST service. The SAL then executes the SPARQL query received from the process engine on the knowledge base. The knowledge base contains domain-specific ontologies describing functionalities of IoT services and devices. Such ontologies define the resource model in this proposal. The result of a query may contain a set of available IoT services that fulfil the properties of the SPARQL query. Subsequently, the IoT services are invoked with the provided semantic command. This is achieved by transforming the semantic command to service calls. Depending on the type of method, either sensor data is retrieved or an actuating command is executed. Finally, the IoT service response is semantically annotated by the SAL and forwarded to the process engine. The semantic service discovery and invocation are realized by the SAL (a more detailed description of this service can be found in Sect. 3.2).

Chun et al. [14] argue that an information model for IoT should be semantically modelled in terms of ontologies defining common terms used in the IoT domain to model resources and exposed services. In this context, they present a discovery service comprising an information model based on ontologies to support semantic description of three components: entities of interest, resources and services. To reflect the dynamics of these IoT components, the proposed information model includes an attribute that indicates whether the component description is static or dynamic. Values of attributes of a description indicated as static do not change with time, e.g. the location of an entity or resource can be static. A dynamic description indicates that the values of the attributes vary often or in an indeterminate way. If a component is declared as dynamic, a new relationship between components can be created or an existing relationship can be removed. Furthermore, to define an interaction between IoT components and the directory that stores the description of these components, the authors proposed the use of two additional values in the information model: passive and active. A passive component indicates that the directory must send a request to get updated information. An active component forwards updated metadata to the directory whenever its metadata changes.

The proposal described in [15] includes a middleware that manages the communication and interoperation among IoT devices. The middleware is responsible for tasks' discovery, and for allocating tasks to objects so as to leverage the resource sharing in the system. The middleware encompasses a semantic layer that adopts semantic technologies for the description of: objects capabilities and characteristics, such as capability to sense temperature or energy consumption to process an instruction; application subdivision into tasks and definition of task characteristics; requirements, such as QoS/QoI (Quality of Information) parameters; network characteristics such as the communication protocol used and objects' deployment. The authors adopt the Semantic Sensor Network (SSN) ontology [12] in the middleware semantic layer to model sensor parameters, resources, services and QoS/QoI related parameters.

3.1.3 Examples of Virtualization-Based Approaches

The concept of virtualization is commonly adopted to hide heterogeneity and complexity of resources, thus facilitating their management and utilization. The core idea in virtualization is to abstract away 'physical resources', which can then be 'composed' at a logical level to support usage by multiple independent users and even by multiple concurrent applications. Resource models in an IoT ecosystem can be built by relying on different levels of virtualization, ranging from simple one-to-one virtualization of single physical devices to virtualization of devices based on complex fusion/aggregation functions. Also, different granularities of virtualization, encompassing devices, group of devices, sub-networks, etc. can be applied. Moreover, since in IoT not only the devices are heterogeneous, but also the (inter) networking schemes and communication protocols, virtualization of the networks and network functions is also required. The virtualized entities of different levels and granularities will compose the resource model.

Some proposals leverage the concept of virtualization to design the so-called virtual sensor networks (VSN) [16]. Building VSNs was motivated mainly by the realization that most of the sensor nodes in a WSN remain idle for most of the time. VSNs are based on two main premises: (i) clearly separating (in terms of organization and management) the physical sensing infrastructure from the virtu-alized entities, which are built upon the physical nodes and (ii) offering services to the applications based on the virtual nodes, sometimes representing aggregations built from multiple physical networks. This approach promotes a better utilization of the system resources. Examples of works adopting the VSN approach are [15], [17] to be discussed later in this book (see Chap. 4). However, these works do not explicitly detail the adopted model to build the virtual representation of a virtual node from existing physical devices. Therefore, they are not discussed in this section.

Another approach strongly built on the concept of virtualization is the software-defined network (SDN) [18]. Several authors have recently adopted the SDN approach to build IoT infrastructures that abstract low-level network com-ponents and functionalities, and enable their provisioning and management through a well-defined high-level API. This allows exposing the underlying infrastructure resources in a set of fine-grained logical components, whose functionality is abstracted way by software and can be provisioned and configured after the deployment of the physical components. While software-defined networks are already a reality in many communication networks, research on sensor network virtualization, which are essential to develop IoT ecosystems, is still in its infancy and comprehensive solutions still need to be found to cope with the specific characteristics of WSNs in terms of limited node capabilities and communication bandwidth. In the next paragraphs, we discuss one example of work that models and manages IoT resources following the paradigm of SDNs.

The authors of [19] go a step beyond several approaches [7, 20] that apply the SDN paradigm in IoT as it is, and propose a new concept called software-defined IoT systems. In their work, the authors cope with the heterogeneity challenge in IoT while providing fine-tuning and customized management for different applications. They argue that a serious drawback of existing solutions to integrate IoT and cloud is the lack of mechanisms to provide flexible and fine-grained customization of IoT com-ponents, hindering the consumption of IoT resources at a finer granularity level. They argue that the limited support for such fine-grained customization at higher levels (application level, for instance), produce tightly coupled and application-specific designs, leading to the need of tedious and error prone configurations at multiple levels of the system. To fulfil this gap, they propose a software-defined IoT system com-prising a set of resource components, hosted in the cloud, which can be provisioned and controlled at runtime. The IoT resources (e.g. sensor generated data streams), their runtime environments (e.g. gateways) and capabilities (e.g. communication proto-cols, analytics and controllers) are described as software-defined IoT units. Such IoT units expose well-defined API and can be composed at different levels, creating virtual runtime topologies on which IoT systems and applications can be deployed and executed. The software-defined IoT units encompass both functional and non-functional aspects of the IoT resources and are configured based on a set of policies. They also support mechanisms to map the virtual resources with the underlying physical infrastructure. The runtime governance API exposed by the units enables performing runtime control operations such as starting or stopping the unit or changing the topological structure of their dependencies. Finally, the units have utility cost-functions that enable pricing the IoT resources as utilities, thus fully exploiting all the benefits of an integrated IoT-cloud system. In their proposal, IoT applications are built by composing together and configuring a set of units, considering the application functional requirements and quality attributes. In this sense, we can consider that their approach includes both a resource and an application model. However, there is no detail about the elements used to describe an application, besides that fact that it is represented by a composition of software-defined units. Their proposal also includes centrally managed configuration models and policies, along with mechanisms to specify and propagate the configuration models to the edge of IoT-cloud infrastructure (e.g. gateways).

3.1.4 Discussion

The described proposals for the resource modelling activity were grouped into three main categories: *attribute-based, semantic-based* and *virtualization-based* (Table 3.1). In this chapter, we review these proposals in the light of three aspects: the degrees of abstraction, granularity and formalism with which the elements are represented in the models.

The first category can be considered the simplest one, since resources are merely described as a set of (low level) attributes. This approach allows for a finer granularity, as attributes describe specific characteristics of device hardware such as CPU, storage capacity or the energy budget. Such characteristics are modelled in terms of what the system is capable of providing. The use of such representation to model the available (physical or virtual) resources in the system determines that the specification of applications is also based on the same format. That is, applications are also modelled in terms of attributes, but in this case describing the resources they require to use from the system. The resource allocation function is essentially responsible for mapping the desired attributes to the available attributes. A formal

Table 3.1 Comparison of approaches for resource modelling

Category	Examples of proposals	Abstraction degree		Granularity		Formalism	
		High	Low	Fine	Coarse	High	Low
Attribute-based approaches	[3–5]		✓	✓		✓	
Semantic-based approaches	[11, 13, 14]	✓		✓	✓	✓	
Virtualization approaches	[7, 15, 17, 19, 20]	✓		✓	✓		✓

model can be built to describe the attributes characterizing resources and applications, thereby imparting a high degree of precision for such proposals.

Regarding the degree of abstraction of these approaches, it can be considered low, since attributes are directly related to physical characteristics of devices. Either there is a one-to-one mapping between the attribute and the physical resource it represents, or a one-to-many in the case of virtual resources, in any case the used elements always refer to low-level attributes of devices. There are no higher level and/or domain-specific elements available to describe the application or its requirements. It can be argued that an IoT user would not need to know exactly how much CPU or memory his/her application needs, not even the power budget required from devices. Functional requirements can be described only in terms of sensor types and geographic location, both information of the user purview. However, the non-functional requirements (QoS) should be able to be expressed in terms, for instance, of minimum life time of the system or maximum delay desired. Approaches based on attributes assume that the system user knows how to map his/her highest level requirements for the lowest level attributes available. Another question about the degree of abstraction is that the attributes are restricted to hardware elements and functionality, but there is no representation for software resources or a view of higher level services. It can be said that in those approaches, the IoT system is basically seen as an infrastructure level provider (as in the IaaS model adopted in cloud systems).

More sophisticated mechanisms for resource modelling are based on using semantic technologies, in general, and ontologies, in particular. Such mechanisms are often adopted by service-oriented approaches and they promote a high abstraction level to represent IoT resources. With such an approach, models can be created from a higher level perspective, and resources can be consumed as a service, not only at the Infrastructure level (IaaS) but also at platform or software levels (Platform as a Service—PaaS and Software as a Service—SaaS—cloud models). Ontologies are based on description logic, thus they inherently provide a high degree of formalism in the resource representation. An ontology is a formal representation of a set of concepts within a domain and of the relationships between those concepts. Ontologies are very expressive and flexible, so they allow representing both hardware and software, physical and virtual resources and in a variety of granularities. Concepts can be defined to model a single IoT device and its physical components, along with the relationships between them (for instance a part of relation). Models of virtual resources representing software components and programmatic functions can be created and related to one or a group of physical devices. Ontology is indeed a powerful mechanism and allows providing the user or the application with a tailored view of the underlying resources, according to the specific needs. In addition, when using ontologies to represent resources, all other Semantic Web tools (as semantic query, discovery and reasoning) are inherited as a bonus and provide solutions to represent applications.

The third category of works consists in virtualization approaches, which can provide a high degree of abstraction to model IoT resources. Such approaches may focus on device virtualization, network virtualization or virtualization of the system as a whole, thus providing different granularities for modelling. In this context, software-defined techniques (SDN) are major mechanisms to abstract low-level components and functionalities (resources), enabling their provisioning and management through high-level and well-defined APIs.

SDN techniques focus on the representation of system elements mainly to support management functions, among which the resource allocation is included. The two basic principles of SDN approaches consist of (i) building an abstraction layer that separates the data plan from the controls plan and hides irrelevant details for each management decision; and (ii) defining a set of policies that guide such decisions, to be performed by the SDN controllers. SDN controllers can be set with different granularities, enabling them to offer different system views and manage components of different levels. For example, controllers can be deployed in sink or cluster nodes in WSNs to control the behaviour of individual nodes or of groups of nodes. Regarding the rigour/precision of the models adopted to represent resources and applications in SDN, the investigated studies do not include any formal specifications or model for this, so we can consider that they have a low degree of formalism. Basically, IoT resources are described as software-defined units and exposed via well-defined APIs. Such software-defined units encompass both functional and non-functional aspects of the IoT resources and are configured based on a set of policies. Applications can access and consume such resources via these APIs, which to a certain extent define rules to be complied with but without enforcing any specific model to build the applications.

3.2 Application Modelling

The upper layer of an IoT resource model refers to how IoT applications are specified. Since this level of modelling is intended to be used by the application developers and/or final users, a high-level language, preferably with visual support, is recommendable for this purpose. In the context of resource allocation, applications are commonly represented as sets of tasks, and tasks are formally represented as directed acyclic graphs (DAGs). Some proposals in the IoT context represent applications based on some sort of structured workflow graphs (SWG) [21]. Following we describe examples of two different approaches, one based on a visual IDE and other based on business process modelling.

3.2.1 Examples of Approaches Based on GUI

The OpenIoT framework, already discussed in the context of resource modelling, also encompasses a set of tools to the visual development of IoT applications and services, as well as for the visual presentation of their results [22]. In OpenIoT, IoT applications are specified as service requests through the request definition tool, which features a graphical user interface (GUI) and comprises a set of functions for specifying and formulating such requests and submitting them to the OpenIoT Global Scheduler. The service modelling provided by the request definition tool uses a graph-based language, where applications are modelled as service graphs, called OSMOs (OpenIoT Service Model Objects). OSMOS specify a real-life application (e.g. weather reports). Service graphs can be grouped together as OpenIoT Application Model Objects (OAMOs) to enable end users to manage (non-related) applications from a single entry point. The metadata describing the modelled services are persisted by the OpenIoT Scheduler and are automatically loaded whenever a user accesses the Web application. The nodes in a service graph are color-coded to indicate its function and provide input and output endpoints defining their accepted connections. Each endpoint belongs to one or more scopes while its position on the rendered node is dictated by its function: inputs on the left and outputs on the right. All service graphs should contain at least one source node (typically a sensor type) and one sink node (a visualization widget) that dictates the flow of information of the application. Data transformation, such as data fusion and/or filtering, can be represented using other node types that can be positioned between the source and the sink. Data source nodes are used to model the sensor types available for querying via the OpenIoT middleware platform. Sensor instances of a particular sensor type at a specific location are modelled as sensor nodes. Selection filter nodes can be connected to sensor nodes to limit the data records that will be processed within a specific time window. Comparator nodes can be connected to a selection filter node to define a time-based filter, for example, the Between Comparator nodes can be used to process only records falling between two specific dates. Group nodes allow users to partition the sensor data into time buckets. A group node is setup by connecting each property of a sensor node (for instance, temperature) that should be grouped to the group node's input endpoint. The partitioned time bucket is represented as a group node endpoint, which can be connected to an aggregation node or directly to a compatible sink node. Aggregation functions (e.g. min, max, count, average and sum) are defined using aggregation nodes. These nodes accept as input the outputs of sensor, groups or aggregation nodes. The termination endpoint of a service graph is indicated by a sink node. All service graphs should have at least one sink node connected to be considered correct. While a standard set of sink nodes is provided, additional sink nodes can be defined depending on the application.

3.2.2 Examples of Approaches Based on Business Process Modelling

Another prominent approach to model IoT application is through business process (BP) modelling [23]. Besides being a well-known approach to abstract the specification of process from their implementation and execution, BP has the value of seamlessly integrate the information generated by the IoT ecosystem with traditional information systems. However, traditional BPs languages are not tailored to deal with streams of events, which are a common paradigm for the representation of information from sources like the IoT or cyber-physical systems. The notion of a stream illustrates that new events occur over time, e.g. continuous temperature sensor readings. In such event-based systems, event producers do not necessarily know the event consumers, or whether the events will be consumed at all. This independence is intrinsic to the event-based approach [24]. The decoupling of event producers and consumers as well as the arrival of an indefinite number of events over time requires an appropriate event dissemination mechanism. Commonly, publish/subscribe systems are used; they allow asynchronous communication between fully decoupled participants. Event consumers specify their interest in events in form of subscriptions; event producers specify the type of events they may publish in advertisements. While single events are a well-known and established concept in BPs [25], event stream processing lacks an appropriate abstraction for the seamless integration across the process modelling, process execution and IT infrastructure layer.

The paper in [23] proposes an infrastructure to seamlessly integrate stream data generated by IoT devices into a workflow engine. Such infrastructure provides a clear separation of concerns between the business perspective and the IT perspective through the concept of *event stream processing units* (SPUs) that encapsulates event stream processing logic, hiding its technical details. SPUs are modelled as event processing tasks (ESPTs), which are abstract representation of business functions that process event streams produced by IoT devices. To make event streams accessible by the modeller, the model introduces the Event Stream Specification (ESS) element, which references a stream of events and their parameter and can be used as input and output of ESPTs. An input ESS defines the subscription an ESPT has to issue, while as used as output it defines the advertised event output stream produced by an ESPT. A key feature of SPUs is the capability of dealing with continuous processing of event streams. Therefore, the model defines constructors to allow ESPTs to run continuously and in parallel to other tasks, including the appropriate execution semantics adapted to event-based characteristics. SPUs require a technical representation to run in a given execution infrastructure. Eventlets are service-like abstraction introduced to address such an issue that encapsulates event stream processing logic with respect to a certain entity. Eventlet instances run in a distributed setting and have a managed lifecycle; application logic can be executed upon instantiation, removal, completion and upon event arrival.

3.2.3   Discussion

The adoption of ontology to represent resources allows using other semantic-based techniques to build applications. For example, an application may be described as a semantic query, which will provide access to the data provided by the IoT system. This is an example of a declarative approach to represent applications. As the user is not always familiar with the syntax of the semantic query languages, IDEs can be provided, allowing easy and friendly access to the system data. In contrast to declarative approaches, programmatic approaches can be used to model IoT applications. An example is the use of workflows, which may or may not contain semantic elements. An interesting work in this line [23] adapts the business process (BP) modelling approach to take into account the specific requirements of IoT, in particular the processing of event streams.

Solutions based on semantic queries, as adopted in OpenIoT [11], are primarily data-driven approaches. Languages like SPARQL provide a wide range of expressions for constructing elaborate and flexible queries and can accommodate a wide range of functional requirements of the applications. The use of IDEs allows direct handling of queries by the end user. The data can be easily viewed and manipulated in various ways using graphic facilities. As for the integration of data with information systems, a new API would have to be built, possibly proprietary, to mediate such integration, so that the data from IoT systems can be consumed directly by external systems. In contrast, BPM-based approaches are more task-oriented than data-driven. Applications are typically modelled as task graphs, and these tasks can be of various types. In query-based approaches, there is no explicit concept of task, although a query for data is implicitly mapped to a sensing task followed by processing and communication. Actuation tasks are not easily represented as in the workflow approaches. In addition, the adoption of an approach based on business process modelling allows seamlessly integrating the information generated by the IoT ecosystem with traditional information systems.

References

1. Oteafy SM, Hassanein HS (2012) Towards a global IoT: resource re-utilization in WSNs. In: Computing, Networking and Communications (ICNC), international conference on, 2012. IEEE, pp 617–622
2. Farias CMD, Li W, Delicato FC, Pirmez L, Zomaya AY, Pires PF, Souza JND (2016) A systematic review of shared sensor networks. ACM Comput Surv (CSUR) 48(4):51
3. Billet B, Issarny V (2014) From task graphs to concrete actions: a new task mapping algorithm for the future Internet of Things. In: 2014 IEEE 11th international conference on mobile ad hoc and sensor systems. IEEE, pp 470–478
4. Angelakis V, Avgouleas I, Pappas N, Fitzgerald E, Yuan D (2015) Allocation of heterogeneous resources of an IoT device to flexible services
5. Sharief M, Kingston O, Hossam S, Kingston O (2012) Resource re-use in wireless sensor networks: Realizing a synergetic internet of things. J Commun 7(7):484–493
6. Banerjee P, Bash C, Friedrich R, Goldsack P, Huberman BA, Manley J, Patel C, Ranganathan P, Veitch A (2011) Everything as a service: powering the new information economy. Computer 44(3):36–43
7. El-Mougy A, Ibnkahla M, Hegazy L (2015) Software-defined wireless network architectures for the Internet-of-Things. In: Local Computer Networks conference workshops (LCN Workshops), IEEE 40th, 2015. IEEE, pp 804–811

8. Whitmore A, Agarwal A, Da Xu L (2015) The Internet of Things—A survey of topics and trends. Inform Syst Frontiers 17(2):261–274

9. Barnaghi P, Wang W, Henson C, Taylor K (2012) Semantics for the Internet of Things: early progress and back to the future. Int J Semant Web Inform Syst (IJSWIS) 8(1):1–21

10. Wang W, De S, Cassar G, Moessner K (2013) Knowledge representation in the internet of things: semantic modelling and its applications. Automatika–J for Control Meas Electron Comput Commun 54(4):388–400

11. Soldatos J, Kefalakis N, Hauswirth M, Serrano M, Calbimonte J-P, Riahi M, Aberer K, Jayaraman PP, Zaslavsky A, Žarko IP (2015) Openiot: open source internet-of-things in the cloud. In: Interoperability and open-source solutions for the Internet of Things. Springer, Berlin, pp 13–25

12. Compton M, Barnaghi P, Bermudez L, GarcíA-Castro R, Corcho O, Cox S, Graybeal J, Hauswirth M, Henson C, Herzog A (2012) The SSN ontology of the W3C semantic sensor network incubator group. Web Semant: Sci Serv Agents World Wide Web 17:25–32

13. Huber S, Seiger R, Schlegel T (2016) Using semantic queries to enable dynamic service invocation for processes in the Internet of Things. In: 2016 IEEE Tenth international Conference on Semantic Computing (ICSC). IEEE, pp 214–221

14. Chun S, Seo S, Oh B, Lee K-H (2015) Semantic description, discovery and integration for the Internet of Things. In: Semantic Computing (ICSC), IEEE international conference on, 2015, pp 272–275

15. Colistra G, Pilloni V, Atzori L (2014) The problem of task allocation in the Internet of Things and the consensus-based approach. Comput Netw 73:98–111

16. Islam MM, Hassan MM, Lee G-W, Huh E-N (2012) A survey on virtualization of wireless sensor networks. Sensors 12(2):2175–2207

17. Delgado C, Gállego JR, Canales M, Ortín J, Bousnina S, Cesana M (2016) On optimal resource allocation in virtual sensor networks. Ad Hoc Netw 50:23–40

18. Xia W, Wen Y, Foh CH, Niyato D, Xie H (2015) A survey on software-defined networking. IEEE Commun Surv Tutorials 17(1):27–51

19. Nastic S, Sehic S, Le D-H, Truong H-L, Dustdar S (2014) Provisioning software-defined iot cloud systems. In: Future Internet of Things and Cloud (FiCloud), international conference on, 2014, pp 288–295

20. Ding J, Yu R, Zhang Y, Gjessing S, Tsang DH (2015) Service provider competition and cooperation in cloud-based software defined wireless networks. IEEE Commun Mag 53 (11):134–140

21. Kiepuszewski B, ter Hofstede AHM, Bussler CJ (2000) On structured workflow modelling. In: International conference on advanced information systems engineering. Springer, Berlin, pp 431–445

22. Kefalakis N, Soldatos J, Anagnostopoulos A, Dimitropoulos P (2015) A visual paradigm for IoT solutions development. In: Interoperability and open-source solutions for the Internet of Things. Springer, Berlin, pp 26–45

23. Appel S, Frischbier S, Freudenreich T, Buchmann A (2013) Event stream processing units in business processes. In: Business process management. Springer, Berlin, pp 187–202

24. Buchmann A, Appel S, Freudenreich T, Frischbier S, Guerrero PE (2012) From calls to events: Architecting future BPM systems. In: International conference on business process management. Springer, Berlin, pp 17–32

25. Van der Aalst WM (1999) Formalization and verification of event-driven process chains. Inf Softw Technol 41(10):639–650

Chapter 4
The Activities of Resource Discovery and Resource Estimation

Abstract In this book, we investigate the core activities encompassed in a holistic resource management process for Internet of Things (IoT), focusing on the different functionalities and architectural approaches involved on a basic workflow for managing the lifecycle of resources in an IoT system. We identified the following activities as the main components of a typical workflow for a resource management system (RMS) in IoT: resource modelling, resource Discovery, resource estimation, resource allocation and resource monitoring. In this chapter, we address the resource discovery and the resource estimation activities. We discuss some challenges regarding these activities in the specific context of IoT and describe existing proposals for them, as a part of a broader resource management solution for IoT ecosystems.

Keywords Internet of Things (IoT) · Resource management · Resource allocation · Resource discovery · Resource estimation

4.1 Resource Discovery in IoT Ecosystems

Allocation of resources in a distributed system requires to be preceded by a process of searching and discovering of the available resources. Services Discovery is a well-studied topic in distributed systems and Web services. Therefore, existing proposals in these two areas can serve as inspiration for the development of IoT services discovery. However, most existing proposals cannot be directly applied to IoT, as they do not satisfy some requirements in this context. According to [1], a major challenge regarding resource discovery in IoT is its ultra large scale. The resources to be discovered may consist of potentially millions of *things* and their produced sensing data. Moreover, these *things* can be mobile or intermittently connected to the network, such dynamism further hindering the discovery process. Besides dealing with the scale and dynamics of IoT systems, some researchers [2] have recently pointed out relevant requirements for a resource discovery mechanism in IoT:

© The Author(s) 2017   33
F.C. Delicato et al., *Resource Management for Internet of Things*,
SpringerBriefs in Computer Science, DOI 10.1007/978-3-319-54247-8_4

1. *Flexible Identification Scheme.* Unlike the traditional Internet, where IP addresses uniquely and globally identify a node in the system, or Web services, where URIs provide a standard framework for identifying and addressing resources, there is still no suitable mechanism to identify IoT resources. Although it is assumed that all IoT devices will be addressed via IP (this is possible by the use of IPv6 [3], although its wide adoption is still an ongoing process), the target of a discovery service is not the device itself, but the resources that it can provide. There is currently no standard for this type of identification. Examples of identifiers used in IoT applications include electronic product code (EPC), Universal Product Code, besides URIs and IPv6 addresses. A proper mechanism for identifying, naming and addressing IoT devices and their provided resources is still an open challenge, aggravated by the mobility issue.

2. *Support for Multiattribute and Range Queries.* The discovery mechanism should be able to handle queries for an exact match of a given identifier, as well as queries containing further qualifying attributes (e.g. location and category). Moreover, besides exact match queries, the mechanism should support a query specifying lower and upper boundaries on a single or multiple attributes.

3. *Context-awareness.* In IoT, the service discovery task can benefit significantly from context-awareness. Context can be considered as any environmental information that can be used to characterize the situation of physical entities that are relevant to the interaction between a user and an application, including the user (him/her) self and the application [4]. Context is typically the location, identity, and state of persons, groups, and computational objects in association with the data provided by devices. Indeed, the ultimate goal of IoT is to build an ecosystem that provides user-oriented and context-aware services [5]. Therefore, it is important to augment the service discovery process and support decision-making actions based on context information. A context-aware service discovery in IoT allows the provision of resources according to the current situation of the user and/or application with minimal human intervention, and facilitates the interpretation of data and machine-to-machine communication (M2M). However, traditional approaches to context-aware Web services discovery are not suitable for IoT because the differences between the real-world services and traditional Web services. Real-world services are exposed by devices that provide the state of entities of the physical world in near real time. Meanwhile, traditional Web services are entirely virtual entities that encapsulate business logic. IoT services are typically deployed on devices with limited computing power, network bandwidth, battery and storage, while traditional Web services are typically deployed on computers without so many restrictions. Finally, IoT services are deployed in highly dynamic environments, where resources and services constantly degrade, disappear and reappear possibly due to intermittent disconnection of wireless networks, device mobility and limited capacities. Finally, it is noteworthy that context information in IoT are inherently imperfect and inconsistent, thus requiring the handling of additional knowledge in terms of quality of context (QoC) [6], e.g. information characterizing the accuracy, precision, completeness and freshness of the achieved data.

Recently, some proposals for service discovery in IoT have emerged, though none fully meets all the aforementioned requirements. In the following Section we review some examples of such proposals.

4.1.1 Examples of Proposals for Resource Discovery in IoT

As a solution to the IoT Resource Management challenge, the paper [7] presents the Device Cloud Framework, which allows users to share and dynamically allocate devices on demand. The framework includes a component called *Device Directory, which acts* as a directory service for device resources. It provides the fundamental data model required to describe devices and represent their lifecycle. Allocation of a device resource is preceded by its discovery and proper identification. Hence, it is necessary that a device is announced to a Device Directory and that its descriptions are made available. Each device being added to the Device Cloud must be registered using a unique ID (per one of the general IoT assumptions). If the *Device Type* is already known, only the *Device Instance* needs to be created. Otherwise, the device vendor must add the *Device Type* and properly link it to *Device Categories* and Platform Modules. Each entity persisted by the Device Directories contains basic properties, like the owner, the operator or the domain it belongs to. Such type of directory and all the steps required to register and announce resources provided devices are typical of any service-based system. The difficulties in the IoT context are the scale of the system, discouraging the use of centralized directories, and the lack of standardization, for instance to identify and describe the resources and devices.

The paper in [8] describes the design of distributed infrastructure that has as primary goal to allow smart things to communicate and cooperate taking into account their spatial distribution and large scale. The proposed infrastructure has the following features: (i) *location aware*: it explores location information to avoid global routing whenever possible and also to enable the provision of context-aware services; (ii) *self-management*: the discovery of smart things by the infrastructure as well as configuration and maintenance work on the infrastructure itself requires minimal manual intervention; (iii) *user-friendliness*: the interfaces used to search for services provided by smart things are easily understandable for both human users and machines. The discovery service of the infrastructure explores the locality of smart things interactions through a hierarchical data structure that interconnect management nodes according to the logical identifiers of the places it covers. On top of this architecture, a scalable look-up mechanism resolves queries on resources. Such a location-aware mechanism also provides load balancing, since queries are automatically routed to away from the overloaded parts of the infrastructure.

As in the Web Services area, the adoption of semantics information is considered by different authors as a key factor to facilitate service discovery, thanks to the augmented, machine interpretable information that semantics provides. The semantic access layer (SAL) of the framework presented in [9] and already discussed in Sect. 3.1.2 of this Book, acts as a discovery service. The framework abstracts device-specific service calls as high-level commands and enables process control-flow adaptation according to IoT service response messages. In the proposed abstraction, sensing and actuation functionalities of IoT entities are represented and accessed via IoT services. Besides IoT services and the SAL, the framework architecture also encompasses a process engine. When a semantic process is executed by the process engine, a SPARQL query is sent to the SAL via a REST service. The SAL executes the SPARQL query received from the process engine on the knowledge base in order to discover the available IoT services. The query result contains a set of available IoT services that fulfill the properties of the SPARQL query. Subsequently, the IoT services are invoked with the provided semantic command. Finally, the response of the IoT service is semantically annotated by the SAL and forwarded to the process engine. Conceptually, the SAL acts as a middleware mediating the process engine and various IoT services. Additionally, the SAL integrates a knowledge base for domain-specific ontologies, which describe functionalities of IoT services and devices.

It is important to mention the OpenIoT [10] platform (see Sect. 3.1) and its contributions to the semantic-based resource discovery process in IoT. The Directory Service is the core component of the OpenIoT framework to the resource discovery process, storing semantically annotated descriptions of all the sensors that are available in the platform. It also provides service-based APIs for registering sensors with the directory and for the lookup of sensors. As mentioned in Sect. 3.1, sensor information is registered using semantically annotated descriptions based on an enhanced version of the W3C SSN ontology. The lookup of sensors is implemented on top of an ontology management system (the open source version of OpenIoT uses Virtuoso [11]) that allows querying the directory service using semantic Web techniques (e.g. SPARQL and RDF). Moreover, the discovery service provides linked sensor data modelling capabilities to facilitate the linking and combination of the data outputs of sensors and other devices.

Khodadadi et al. [12] propose a framework, named Simurgh, for the definition, discovery and composition of things and their services. The framework builds upon RAML [13], a REST-based API definition language, extending the language to encompass the definition of IoT objects. Using REST, the process of service discovery and advertising is kept simple and practical. The framework encompasses a Things Layer, a Platform Layer and an End Use Layer. Things Layer includes the Network Discovery and Registration Broker, a component responsible for handling incoming requests from devices that want to join the system. It also keeps a repository of entities with their assigned unique identifiers. The Platform Layer keeps a Thing Description Repository, containing the description of things along with services provided by them. This repository is constantly updated by the Network Discovery and Registration Broker component. Moreover, the Two-Phase Discovery Engine component of the Platform Layer allows discovering "things" that are able to meet the user request, and are also equipped with APIs that can be utilized in a complete data flow to satisfy user requirements. Therefore, the goal of the discovery component is not only finding an entity able to satisfy the desired functional requirements (for instance, in terms of the type of data to be sensed, geographical location and sampling rate) but also endowed with the required API.

Finally, the framework proposed in [12] addresses the scalability issue of IoT by employing the same idea of DNS systems in the Internet and separates the connection requests received from the users according to the domain. The network discovery module registers and keeps the information of all devices connecting to a specific domain. To cope with the heterogeneity of IoT, the framework allows devices using multiple communication protocols such as Bluetooth, ZigBee and Wi-Fi to register themselves and obtain a unique identifier in the IoT system. Upon joining the system, each entity is required to submit a description document with the assigned unique identifier, so that the discovery module is able to know which entities are active and their provided services. The authors claim that it is necessary to create descriptor files to properly describe the main building blocks of an IoT environment, including devices, sensors and humans [12]. Such document must encompass the functional properties of the entities and also their set of callable services. Ideally, a lightweight human-and machine-readable file format should be used to simplify writing descriptions without adding extra overhead. However, due to the lack of standardization in the IoT field, the authors developed their own metamodel to this end. The proposed model is called thing description document (TDD) and specified as a JSON file. A TDD file has two main parts: one to describe properties of the IoT entity and other to describe the services offered by the entity (its API). A simple two-phase syntax-based discovery approach is proposed for efficient discovery of things and their available services. The discovery module searches the TDD repository for entities matching a given criterion. The user can require an exact match or a subsume match when submitting a query [14]. After the initial step of finding entities of interest, a second step queries their provided APIs.

4.1.2 Discussion on Resource Discovery for IoT

A typical discovery process is twofold. First, it is necessary to identify and locate the device (physical or virtual), then it is necessary to find the resource or service provided by the device, which will be effectively used. However, unlike what happens in the traditional Internet, IoT users and applications, in general, are not interested in accessing a particular node in the network, but instead in the resource it provides. The IoT fits well in the concept of content-oriented networks, and as such, the naming and addressing mechanisms should preferably refer to descriptions of resources (or content). However, the current Internet is still heavily based on traditional addressing and naming schemes like IP and URI and a mapping process is always required. In addition to the new IPv6 version, whose adoption lays one of the groundings for the emergence of IoT, there are other schemes being proposed to identify devices and sensors. In the works investigated in this survey, several authors [7] assume that the IoT devices have indeed a unique identifier, such as an IP or MAC address, but this is not a consensus or a premise of all proposals.

In semantic approaches in general the discovery process is converted to a process of semantic query performed on a group of attributes that describe the resource (or service). Devices publish descriptions of their resources in a repository which is queried by the application or user. There is a mapping process to the actual address of these devices which is transparent to the user and/or application and the proposals do not detail this process. In these works, there is no explicit mention of the existence of a globally unique identifier for the device. The focus is always on how to describe/represent resources so that they can be discovered based on attributes that describe them.

Most of the retrieved works considers the possibility of multiattribute queries, but we did not find the studies that support range queries. This type of support is typical in data stream processing systems, but as this is not the focus of the survey, specific papers of this area that do not address resource management have not been retrieved. Regarding the need for context-awareness, retrieved works as [8] mainly consider the location information as relevant contextual data. The use of this type of information can make the discovery process much more efficient both in terms of response time to the users and of the consumption of system resources. Information regarding the quality of context (QoC) was not considered in the analyzed works.

Finally, it is a consensus among the proposals that, in order to deal with the huge scale of IoT, any effective solution for resource discovery should be distributed and should require minimal human intervention.

Table 4.1 summarizes the proposals according to the IoT specific requirements for service discovery as proposed in [2]. It is noticeable that none of the works discussed here fully addressed the considered requirements. However, it is important to mention that the studies analyzed in this Book pertain to the generic context of resource management for IoT, not to the specific context of resource discovery. There are few recent works, mainly in the field of service-oriented middleware for IoT, that propose discovery mechanisms tailored for the specific features of IoT. It has been a common approach to adopt a service-oriented design for building IoT systems. Service-oriented architecture (SOA [15]) has several features that are suitable for IoT, such as the decoupling of components, thus fitting well the dynamic context, and the abstraction of the provided functionalities as

Table 4.1 Comparison of approaches for resource discovery

Papers	Flexible identification scheme	Support for multiattribute and range queries	Context-awareness
[7]	✓ (Unique ID)		✓ (Location-aware)
[8]		✓ (Hierarchical logical identifiers)	
[9]	✓ (Semantic-based)	✓ (Semantic query)	
[10]	✓ (Semantic-based)	✓ (Semantic query)	
[12]	✓ (Name, unique ID, protocol-specific unique ID)	✓ (Subsume matching)	✓ (Domain-aware)

services with well-defined interfaces, thus tackling heterogeneity issues. Moreover, some authors such as [16] claim that the utility and efficiency of IoT applications will heavily depend on the cooperation of heterogeneous IoT devices among themselves and also with information systems. The adoption of a SOA approach naturally aids the integration of physical devices into existing enterprise information systems.

In service-oriented IoT, the starting point for the process of service provisioning is to abstract *things* or their measurements as services. Traditional SOA considers three main actors (or roles) that interact directly with one another: a Service Provider, a Service Consumer and a Registry. Besides these actors, any SOA-based middleware encompasses three core functionalities: Discovery, Composition of, and Access to services [1]. Therefore, middleware for IoT that adopts a service-oriented approach naturally includes some solution for service discovery, which can be regarded as a process for resource discovery (with a service-based resource model). However, most of them only directly apply traditional discovery mechanisms, without considering the IoT particularities. One exception is Hydra [17], former LinkSmart IoT middleware (https://linksmart.eu), which encompasses a mechanism for the discovery of resource-constrained resources. Another example is [18], where the authors specifically address the scale and mobility features of IoT and propose MobIoT, a service-oriented IoT middleware that adopts a novel probabilistic discovery protocol. In MobIoT, both the Registration and Look-up functionalities of the Discovery Component are probabilistic, and the rationale behind that approach is that in a high scale and dynamic scenario as IoT, only a subset of willing providers should be allowed to register their services, depending on whether the already registered ones are sufficient for the consumer. Proposals for IoT middleware are not the focus of our study. Therefore, the research gap identified in our investigation concerns the fact that the activity of resource discovery is still poorly addressed as part of a holistic solution for resource management in IoT.

4.2   Resource Estimation in IoT Ecosystems

Techniques for resource estimation have been investigated in the context of cloud computing, as part of the resource provisioning phase, as a way of assuring the quality of service for the applications. This is particularly relevant for data streams applications requiring real-time processing, which pose strict guarantees on quality of services. According to the authors in [19], having resource usage estimation for processing continuous queries over data streams is vital, yet challenging in cloud systems due to variability of the data arrival rates and their distribution models (e.g. Logistic, Rayleigh), variable resource consumption behaviour of continuous queries, the need of processing different types of continuous queries and uncertainties of the underlying cloud environment. The authors in [20] define resource estimation as a "close guess of the actual resources required for an application", usually with some thought or calculation involved. In this chapter, we consider that, in the context of a RMS, the goal of the resource estimation activity is to prepare the system in advance to accommodate the workload of an arriving application so that its quality requirements are fulfilled. This should be done, preferably, without degrading the quality of already executing applications.

In the following section, we present examples of existing proposals tackling this activity. It is important to mention that the presented studies were retrieved in a context aiming to investigate the resource management problem in general. We did not investigate the literature searching for works specifically targeting resource estimation, but instead works that consider such activity as part of a workflow for resource management in IoT.

4.2.1   Examples of Proposals for Resource Estimation in IoT

The authors in [21] present a service-oriented resource management model for IoT systems supported by Fog, which can help achieving an efficient, effective and fair management of resources. Their proposal for resource estimation was firstly presented in [22] and then leveraged in this work, for the new scenario in consideration, namely an IoT-Fog integrated system. Their work is mainly focused on considering different types of customers and device-based resource estimation and pricing, even in presence of mobility. In their proposed fog-based IoT resource management model, sensors, IoT nodes, devices and cloud service customers (CSCs) contact the Fog to acquire the required service(s) at best price. So, the Fog is the entry point for applications in their proposal. CSCs perform the negotiation and define the service level agreement (SLA) with the Fog. Once the contract is agreed upon, the service is provided to the customer. The Fog is in charge of estimating the consumption of resources, so that they can be allocated in advance. The authors consider that service requests can be made from objects or WSN nodes as well as from devices operated by people. Therefore, prediction and pre-allocation of resources also depend upon user's behaviour and the probability of using those resources in the future.

The authors then present their formulation for the resources estimation, which is very similar to the one presented in [22]. They formulate the estimation of required resources (CPU, memory, storage and bandwidth) as a function of the basic price of the service (negotiated during the establishment of the service provision agreement) and the relinquish probabilities. For simplicity, they categorized customers into two types, one having low (L) probability of giving up a contracted service and the other having high (H) giving up probability. CSCs, in particular mobile users, can have a highly fluctuating behaviour regarding the utilization of resources, which may lead to deception while making decisions about resource allocation. That is the main motivation behind the inclusion, in their model, of the variance of relinquishes probabilities, which helps determining the actual behaviour of each customer. The proposed model includes a constant decision variable value, which is assigned by the Fog resource manager to each user, according to CSC's historical record of overall relinquish probabilities. Most recent behaviour is determined from the last relinquish probability. For new users, without previous data, this value is set at a default low relinquish probability of 0.3. Another element of their formulation represents the type of accessing device. For representing devices, their resources and requirements, an interesting feature in the proposed model formulation regards the representation of the accessing devices for multimedia services. The authors consider that for such type of service, the display size of the device is a relevant parameter, since resources must be allocated according to the specific size and appropriate required quality. The mobility of the devices is also taken into account in a peculiar way in the model. They consider that a mobile device would require more resources from the Fog, since it is in motion and requires quick response. Relatively more resources are required in this case, so that efficient transcoding and data delivery is possible even in presence of motion. It is important to notice that a device such as a laptop can be used in both static and mobile modes. So, in their model the author considers the current mode the device is being used, to avoid wasting resources of the data centres in case the mobility is always assumed for a potentially mobile device. Based on a set of real experiments conducted in different wired and wireless networks (broadband, WiFi, WiBro, 3G and 4G LTE-A), the authors concluded that smartphone and similar devices would require approximately 1.25 of the resources reserved for static device (desktop computer or laptop in static mode). On the other hand, larger mobile device (tablet and laptop) requires approximately 1.5 times of such resources.

An ongoing service can be discontinued at any time by the customer. This is more frequent with customers acceding from mobile and handheld devices. When the service is discontinued, the Fog has to halt the service and refund the remaining amount to the customer. In this case, a refunding value is computed, considering the utilized resources or consumed services and the remaining service value of the decided total initial service. The proposed model also incorporates the concept of incentive for a better customer, since the customers who have used more services generate more profit for the system. When they quit the service, they are provided with some appreciation amount while refunding. On the other hand, a Depreciation Index is applied when resource utilization is less than 60%. This index deducts some amount, based on business policy, from those customers who used very little the contracted service.

In [23] the authors consider the Fog as a layer composed of micro-data centres (MDC) lying between the IoT devices and the mega data centre in the cloud, whose purpose is to manage resources, perform data filtering, pre-processing and security functions. To achieve its goals, Fog requires an effective and efficient resource management framework, which they depict in the paper, however, focusing on the resource estimation activity. They consider the presence of mobile nodes and IoT devices, encompassing objects and devices of different types with a fluctuating connectivity behaviour. The service customers accessing the system from such devices have an unpredictable relinquish probability, since any object or device can stop using resources at any moment. Therefore, in their proposed methodology for resource estimation and management through Fog computing, they take into account these factors and formulate resource management on the basis of fluctuating relinquish probability of the customer, service type, service price and variance of the relinquish probability. In a previous work of the same group [24], the authors proposed a basic mathematical model for resource estimation for Fog computing. In this new paper, they initially extended their model to include a customer's probabilistic resource estimation (PRE) model, with the goal of aiding in efficient, effective and fair management of resources for IoT devices. In the same way as [21], the focus of their work is mainly on estimating the resource consumption based of different types (behaviour) of customers. The main contribution of this new work is the validation of the proposed model with real data traces in an implementation based on the Amazon EC2 data storage pricing. For modelling the customer's characteristics, one of the main components is the service relinquish probability, computed based on the overall record of all the services a customer has been consuming as well as the record for a particular service. In this way, resources are reserved based on that record, which helps minimizing resource underutilization.

In the architecture considered in the paper, the Fog layer includes one or more Fog Smart gateway(s)—FSG—able to handle data communications in a smarter way on the basis of the requirement of the higher level applications and constraints of the underlying devices. Based on the feedback from the application and depending upon the constraints of the node generating data, the FSG decides the timing and type of data to be processed in the Fog and then sent to the cloud. The underlying IoT devices and networks are not always physical. Virtual sensors and VSNs are also required for various services.

4.2.2   Discussion on Resource Estimation for IoT

As aforementioned, the goal of the resource estimation activity is to prepare the system in advance to properly accommodate the workload of an arriving application so that its quality requirements are fulfilled, while preferably not degrading the quality of already executing applications. However, some authors claim that in IoT systems, since there are concurrent applications with multiple priorities (criticalities), it is important to have some kind of pre-emptive mechanism. In this case, higher priority applications can receive their required resources even if lower priority applications are degraded. The investigated approaches make use of the user past behaviour (regarding their resource consumption) and the probability of repeating such behaviour in the future to make the estimation. Therefore, the monitoring activity is required, in order to learn and register such behaviour. Regarding the proposed estimation models themselves, the few retrieved works consider as important factors the actual use of the allocated resources and the probability of service relinquish.

References

1. Issarny V, Bouloukakis G, Georgantas N, Billet B (2016) Revisiting service-oriented architecture for the IoT: a middleware perspective. In: International conference on service-oriented computing. Springer, Berlin, pp 3–17
2. Paganelli F, Parlanti D (2012) A DHT-based discovery service for the Internet of Things. J Comput Netw Commun 2012, Article ID 107041, p 11
3. Deering SE (1998) Internet protocol, version 6 (IPv6) specification. https://tools.ietf.org/html/rfc2460
4. Abowd GD, Dey AK, Brown PJ, Davies N, Smith M, Steggles P (1999) Towards a better understanding of context and context-awareness. In: International symposium on handheld and ubiquitous computing. Springer, Berlin, pp 304–307
5. Wei Q, Jin Z (2012) Service discovery for Internet of Things: a context-awareness perspective. In: Proceedings of the fourth Asia-Pacific symposium on internetware. ACM, p 25
6. Brézillon P, Gonzalez AJ (2014) Context in computing: a cross-disciplinary approach for modeling the real world. Springer
7. Kliem A, Kao O (2015) The Internet of Things resource management challenge. In: 2015 IEEE international conference on data science and data intensive systems. IEEE, pp 483–490
8. Mayer S, Guinard D, Trifa V (2012) Searching in a web-based infrastructure for smart things. In: Internet of Things (IoT), 2012 3rd international conference on the IEEE, pp 119–126
9. Huber S, Seiger R, Schlegel T (2016) Using semantic queries to enable dynamic service invocation for processes in the Internet of Things. In: 2016 IEEE tenth International Conference on Semantic Computing (ICSC). IEEE, pp 214–221
10. Kim J, Lee J-W (2014) OpenIoT: an open service framework for the Internet of Things. In: 2014 IEEE World Forum on Internet of Things (WF-IoT). IEEE, pp 89–93
11. Erling O (2012) Virtuoso, a hybrid RDBMS/graph column store. IEEE Data Eng Bull 35 (1):3–8
12. Khodadadi F, Dastjerdi AV, Buyya R (2015) Simurgh: a framework for effective discovery, programming, and integration of services exposed in IoT. In: International conference on IEEE, Recent Advances in Internet of Things (RIoT), pp 1–6
13. Workgroup R (2015) RAML-RESTful API modeling language. URl: http://raml.org/ (visited on 12/04/2014)
14. Klusch M, Fries B, Sycara K (2006) Automated semantic web service discovery with OWLS-MX. In: Proceedings of the fifth international joint conference on Autonomous agents and multiagent systems. ACM, pp 915–922
15. Lublinsky B (2007) Defining SOA as an architectural style. Estados Unidos IBM Developers 4(1):1
16. Guinard D, Trifa V, Karnouskos S, Spiess P, Savio D (2010) Interacting with the soa-based Internet of Things: discovery, query, selection, and on-demand provisioning of web services. IEEE Trans Serv Comput 3(3):223–235
17. Eisenhauer M, Rosengren P, Antolin P (2010) Hydra: a development platform for integrating wireless devices and sensors into ambient intelligence systems. In: The Internet of Things. Springer, pp 367–373
18. Hachem S, Pathak A, Issarny V (2014) Service-oriented middleware for large-scale mobile participatory sensing. Pervasive Mob Comput 10:66–82
19. Khoshkbarforoushha A, Ranjan R, Gaire R, Jayaraman PP, Hosking J, Abbasnejad E (2015) Resource usage estimation of data stream processing workloads in datacenter clouds. arXiv preprint arXiv:150107020
20. Manvi SS, Shyam GK (2014) Resource management for Infrastructure as a Service (IaaS) in cloud computing: a survey. J Netw Comput Appl 41:424–440
21. Aazam M, Huh E-N (2015) Fog computing micro datacenter based dynamic resource estimation and pricing model for IoT. In: 2015 IEEE 29th international conference on advanced information networking and applications. IEEE, pp 687–694

22. Aazam M, Huh E-N (2014) Resource management in media cloud of things. In: 2014 43rd international conference on parallel processing workshops, IEEE, pp 361–367
23. Aazam M, St-Hilaire M, Lung C-H, Lambadaris I (2016) PRE-Fog: IoT trace based probabilistic resource estimation at fog. In: 2016 13th IEEE annual Consumer Communications & Networking Conference (CCNC). IEEE, pp 12–17
24. Aazam M, Huh E-N (2015) Dynamic resource provisioning through fog micro datacenter. In: IEEE international conference on Pervasive Computing and Communication Workshops (PerCom Workshops). IEEE, pp 105–110

Chapter 5
The Activity of Resource Allocation

Abstract In this chapter, we address the resource allocation, which is the main activity in a holistic resource management process for Internet of Things (IoT) ecosystems. We discuss existing approaches that tackle the challenges of providing a resource allocation system for the IoT. We focus our discussion on works addressing the challenges from an architectural point of view, proposing the main components involved in the resource allocation activity along with their functionalities and operation. Existing proposals differ in several aspects, but in this chapter, we group them according to the number of tiers involved in the resource allocation. First, we discuss works focused on the cloud tier, in which the main players in the allocation process are the virtualized data centres at the cloud. In such proposals, the IoT devices are passive entities only in charge of producing data to be processed at the cloud. Then, we discuss approaches that distribute the workload between the IoT devices and the cloud. Following, we present the proposals in which the main players in the resource allocation process are the IoT devices themselves, the so-called IoT only approached. Finally, we briefly present works that exploit resource utilization at the edge of the network, thus adopting a three-tier architecture for IoT and dealing with the allocation process considering these three tiers, with their distinct features.

Keywords Internet of Things (IoT) · Resource management · Resource allocation · Cloud computing · Cloud of things · Edge computing

5.1 Overview of Resource Allocation in IoT

In cloud computing, resource allocation has the main goal of guaranteeing the satisfaction of application requirements by using the cloud resources, while minimizing the overall operational cost. Resource allocation in IoT has a similar goal, with further requirements introduced by the new players and the specific nature of data produced by IoT devices, characterized as data streams. New players are the things (IoT devices) and intermediary nodes such as gateways/smart gateways/fog/edge devices. By introducing such devices, which are able to receive and process the application workload along with cloud nodes (whenever they are present in the IoT system), a new level of complexity arises in the allocation decision. Depending on the application specific needs in terms of processing load or response time, nodes at different tiers in a three-tier IoT system are more suitable to be assigned. Cloud nodes can provide complex data analytics, based on historical data, and they can serve as a long-term repository for both raw and processed data. Nodes at the edge of the network, on the other hand, allow real-time delivery of data, required for emergency, health care, and other latency sensitive IoT applications. Moreover, edge/fog nodes have some features such as location-awareness and mobility that are not present in traditional cloud nodes. Finally, although more constrained in resources, the IoT devices (things) are able to provide some simple processing for real-time applications, either individually or collaboratively, without resourcing to remote nodes from other tiers. Such capabilities cannot be ignored to fully utilize the resources available in the system and satisfy application needs.

The new dimensions of heterogeneity and dynamism, along with the aforementioned aspects of an IoT system, make the resource allocation a highly complex and challenging task that requires novel solutions to design a resource allocation system (RAS) tailored to this scenario. A RAS for IoT needs to deal with unpredictable requests from applications in an elastic and transparent way and exploiting the diverse nature and opportunistic offer of resources. This elasticity should allow the dynamic use of physical resources, avoiding both the under-provisioning and over provisioning of resources.

As aforementioned, the main goal of a RAS is assuring the proper meeting of application requirements by the infrastructure, while minimizing its operational cost. Additional goals include: load balance, whereby resources should be allocated in a manner so that utilization is balanced across all resources of a particular type; fault tolerance, whereby resources are allocated in a manner such that the impact of a failure of individual components does not compromise the overall system performance, among others [1].

In this chapter, we discuss existing approaches that tackle the challenges of providing such a RAS. We focus our discussion on works addressing the challenges from an architectural point of view, proposing the main components involved in the resource allocation activity along with their functionalities and operation. Some works include, beside the main architectural building blocks of a RAS, algorithmic solutions, by modelling the resource allocation problem and formulating solutions for it based on well-known theoretical frameworks. In our analysis, we emphasize the architectural point of view, since we are interested in discussing the main activities and functional building blocks of a resource management layer (RML, see Chap. 2).

Some proposals assume a three-tier architecture for IoT ecosystems, where the lower tier encompasses the things or IoT devices, the top tier is a cloud system and the intermediary tier is composed of a set of interconnected gateways or fog/edge nodes. Those approaches are the most heterogeneous and complex ones in terms of the computational entities involved, and they open several possibilities on how to efficiently manage the available resources. Some works do not consider the cloud tier, but only the things and one or more gateways. These gateways have various degrees of complexity and responsibilities in terms of resource management. On the other hand, some proposals do not assume the presence of the edge nodes, only things and the cloud (eventually some gateway node intermediates the communication but without any complex task other than acting as a relay node). Finally, there are works that consider only the resources provided by the things and how to efficiently manage them to meet application requests. In this latter category, there are recent works considering the specific features of IoT devices, which we will discuss in more depth, and also works derived from the WSN field, and although we will briefly discuss them, they are not the focus of this book. However, there are works that discuss the challenges of adapting WSN design and operation to effectively integrate with IoT systems. Such proposals are within the scope of our discussion.

In the remainder of this chapter, we organize the description of existing proposals according to the tier in which the resource allocation decision takes place.

5.2 Cloud Only Approaches

In this section, we will describe works that consider the integration of IoT devices with the cloud with the main purpose of sharing device resources/data via virtualization techniques. In such proposals, IoT devices are passive data sources, and all the processing and storage functions are executed in the cloud data centres.

5.2.1 Examples of Cloud Only Approaches

An example of proposal for resource allocation in IoT focused on the cloud is described in [2]. The authors propose a solution to optimize the deployment of RFID applications using cloud computing. They consider IoT applications as being built only upon RFID data, instead of encompassing data produced from a more heterogeneous set of devices. They claim that, for efficiently deploying RFID applications on the cloud, an important issue is to address the 'flows' of RFID tags between RFID readers and their client applications. The authors consider a flow as a stream of tags coming from RFID readers; these flows are created when tags are detected in the vicinity of a reader's antenna and sent to clients. They address the problem of managing how flows produced by an unknown number of incoming tags are processed by a set of virtual machines (VMs) in the cloud. Since the exact capacity and timing of each flow in a given RFID reader are unknown, there will be fluctuations in the VM loads. Whenever a VM experiences overloads, some flows should be migrated, thus sending tags to other VMs. However, two main challenges need to be tackled to support this migration procedure. First, since flows have TCP connections, employing direct TCP-based migrations would introduce overhead as well as changes to TCP state machines [2]. When the number of flows needed to be migrated increases to thousands of flows, the overhead will become unacceptable. Second, there is a need for an efficient strategy to manage the migration performance inside the cloud, including decisions on when, where, and what to migrate.

In order to tackle the identified challenges, the authors designed and implemented a prototype system focusing on optimized load balancing for RFID application deployments on cloud. To achieve their goals, they proposed strategies for load prediction and flows migration among VMs, encompassing all the steps required for effective migration management (when, where, and what to migrate). Their proposed architecture has two main components: a load predictor and a migration manager. The load predictor is responsible for predicting future loads from historical values of VMs' load. Besides predicting effects of migration delay, this component also allows the cloud system to know VMs' future loads and their stabilization time after migration. The migration manager decides whether to make flow migrations for any overloading VMs based on the load predictor's prediction results [2]. The load predictor and the migration manager are the main components of the controller subsystem. The proposed architecture also encompasses two other groups of components, namely the CloudStack Management Software & Hosts and RFID Readers. Whenever the controller decides that migrations need to be performed, a migration list is created, and then this list is executed by the CloudStack management software.

The core of the load predictor component is a prediction algorithm. For a prediction algorithm based on past statistics to perform well, strong correlation between past and future statistics is necessary. In the proposed system, this correlation depends on flows received from RFID readers, including the number of flows and the number of tags from each flow during each observed interval. As a result, whenever a group of flows is migrated out of a VM, this correlation relation is weakened; thus, those statistics are considered outdated and no longer used for prediction. As the proposed migration strategy consists of gradually migrating flows out of VMs, this means only limited amount of statistics is available between consecutive migrations; therefore, prediction algorithms that require a training phase (i.e. Linear Autoregression) would not be a suitable choice. Considering such issues, the authors adopted the exponential moving average (EMA) algorithm for the predictions made by the load predictor.

Regarding the migration decision, to properly perform flow migrations for VMs, three key issues need to be addressed, including (i) which flows to migrate, (ii) when to migrate, and (iii) where to migrate them. To tackle the first issue, it is necessary to calculate the amount of CPU the migrated flows would take inside the destination VM, which is not a trivial and straightforward calculation. The authors estimate this value by using the ratio of migrated tags to total tags with the source VM's load value. Regarding the migration time, they adopt a reactive approach in which the system performs flow migrations whenever a situation of overloading is detected. A VM is defined to be in overloading situation if the resources utilization (e.g. CPU, memory) exceeds a predefined threshold for a predefined amount of time. Moreover, flow migrations are performed only if the source VM currently has no migration delay effect. Finally, for deciding about the migration destination, it is chosen to be the VM with the highest load value that can receive the migrated flows of tags without turning into an overloading VM itself.

The work proposed in [2] considers only RFIDs as IoT devices. However, the heterogeneity of objects that are part of the IoT ecosystem is one of its main features. Among the plethora of things that can integrate the IoT, an important category consists on the various mobile devices such as smart phones, smart TVs, tablets, etc. The combination of cloud computing, mobile computing and wireless networks gave rise to the recent paradigm of *mobile cloud computing (MCC)* [3]. MCC aims to provide augmented computational resources to mobile users, network operators and cloud computing providers. MCC enables the execution of rich mobile applications on a myriad of mobile devices, providing the user with value-added services that exploits mobility and the context awareness resource provisioning. Although IoT and MCC are two distinct paradigms, designed from different perspectives, and investigated in different research fields, they have many similarities. In particular, both consider the interconnection of smart devices to provide innovative and context-aware services for the end user. Therefore, we include some examples of works from the MCC field in our discussion on resource allocation in cloud integrated IoT ecosystems.

In this context, the authors in [4] investigate the field of the so-called geo-distributed mobile cloud computing (GMCC). GMCC denotes an emergent scenario that adds geography issues in MCC [5]. The presence of high mobility of nodes, for instance when considering applications running from vehicles, poses a significant challenge to maintain a stable network topology as well as providing reliable resources. In such scenario, centralized data centre infrastructures have several disadvantages, including limited resource sharing, high bandwidth for communications and long distance to users. In GMCC, the cloud resource and data centres are geographically distributed over a wide-area network in order to satisfy ever-increasing computing requirements for mobile users in a large area [5]. In this scenario, each data centre is mainly responsible for users in its neighbourhood. Considering the devices mobility, the execution of a given application may span for a large geographical region, thus involving different data centres to meet its requests. Therefore, a cooperation scenario emerges. In [4] the authors address resource sharing through cooperation among service providers (SPs) in GMCC. They exploit the cooperation among SPs, where resource rich SPs are encouraged to lease a portion of their resource to the resource-deficient SPs, in order to increase the overall resource utilization. They formulate the resource cooperation among SPs using the coalition game theory framework and then leverage pricing mechanism and users demand to stimulate the cooperation. They optimize the VMs migration and resource allocation to deal with the mobility issues. The authors employ graph theory (with a 2-layer graph) in order to compute the global optimization.

Since the computation part of mobile Internet applications can be offloaded to the powerful servers in the cloud for various purposes, the cloud service providers (CSPs) conform to a virtual resource network. It provides CPU, memory and bandwidth resources in order to support such applications. The coalition game in this GMCC network promotes resource cooperation either among the local SPs or remote SPs. The local resource cooperation focuses on sharing the available resources between different SPs in the same datacentre, and the remote resource cooperation focused on sharing the available resources of the same SP between different datacentres [4]. The goal of the resource cooperation is to balance the extreme unbalance of SPs resource utilization so that the revenue can be improved by increasing the resource utilization appropriately. To prevent the overutilization of the resource that could reduce QoS significantly, the authors also introduced the penalty function to avoid the resource to be shared greedily. In other words, once the penalty function is triggered, the SP will refuse the newly arrival applications until it has enough resource for processing them.

Both over-an underutilization of resources is not desirable for the cloud providers and consumers. Two major goals of CSPs are maintaining high resource utilization of cloud computing resources while increasing revenues. Another goal, whose relevance has recently increased, following the trend of building greener and more sustainable systems, is keeping energy costs low. In order to achieve the two former goals, resource overbooking techniques are often employed [6–9], in which more resources, such as CPU and memory, are committed than are actually available on the physical machines. Statistical multiplexing is the key concept behind the overbooking strategy. In the same way, statistical multiplexing is commonly used in data networks to exploit the bursty nature of the traffic, the intuition behind its employment in cloud is the fact that users of traditional cloud applications often request more resources than their applications actually need and almost never at the same time. This feature creates an opportunity to the cloud provider to overbook resources. However, as the authors discuss in [10], the unpredictable arrival pattern of data stream-based IoT applications makes it hard to estimate the number of requested resources. Therefore, statistical multiplexing may not be as effective for such applications, and resource overbooking may adversely impact the application performance. This adverse impact is a consequence of the lack of complete isolation between the operations of collocated VMs. However, as the authors claim in [10], there is no perfect solution to provide a virtualized environment totally free from performance interference between VMs [11, 12]. They argue that tackling the challenges of performance interference derived from resource overbooking while satisfying the performance and response time requirements of IoT applications requires managing the trade-offs in the placement of VMs on host machines by carefully considering the actual workload characteristics of the VMs [10]. The high dynamism intrinsic of IoT application workloads along with the tendency of VMs to migrate from one physical machine to another for a variety of reasons, make traditional offline heuristics such as bin packing not suitable for interference-aware VM placement in such environment.

Consequently, to provide a solution for such a challenge, the authors proposed a system architecture that encompasses a component for monitoring variations in the performance interference along with a VM placement strategy [10]. Their solution takes into account both the effects of performance interference and the workload characteristics of the collocated VMs on the target host machine. In their work, a middleware called iSensitive is proposed to be deployed in IoT cloud back-ends. Such middleware is in charge of performing the online monitoring of performance interference. The differences in performance between the BASE, non-overbooked, and overbooked environments are compared and the impact of resource utilization on performance interference is then analyzed. Using the outcome of this analysis process, a machine-learning method is employed to learn about the desired VM placement patterns. Such patterns are then used in the iSensitive middleware to make runtime decisions on VM placement.

iSensitive is a cloud back-end resource management middleware tailored for IoT applications, thus tackling the unpredictability of the arrival patterns of such applications. In order to estimate the patterns of incoming workloads, iSensitive adopts a model predictive approach based on learning from historical data regarding the resource utilization. The online monitoring process performed by iSensitive provides high quality and fine-grained historical data that allows building an accurate model of the system subsequently used for runtime decisions of VM placement.

The authors in [13] address a very relevant aspect of resource allocation for IoT, namely the different priorities of IoT applications. In the inherently heterogeneous IoT systems, service expectations and requirements of a health application are naturally much higher than those of and application to keep the users comfortable in a room. Therefore, scheduling algorithms must consider different priorities for different classes of applications when handling the user requests. In this context, the authors first claim that current cloud servers are not well prepared to deal with such requirement of IoT, for several reasons. One interesting point discussed in their paper regards the homogeneity versus heterogeneity of cloud servers in terms of the provided service rates, among other parameters. In order to properly tackle the discussed challenge, the authors propose a novel cloud server scheduling algorithm by considering priority classes of IoT requests. The level of priority for an application request is used to decide the next request to be served and allocate the amount of resources for each request. They assume the presence of homogeneous and heterogeneous servers in the cloud system and also of both shared and dedicated servers. Their main contributions are the proposal of two schemes, namely the homogeneous dynamic dedicated server scheduling (DDSS) and the heterogeneous dynamic dedicated server scheduling (h-DDSS) along with the detailed explanation of the scheduling procedure. Moreover, they provide a comprehensive analysis (both theoretical and via simulations) of a cloud system using their approaches in terms of throughput, drop rate, and utilization.

5.2.2 Discussion

The focus of the proposals presented in Sect. 5.2 was in adapting cloud platforms to deal with the novel demands of IoT scenarios. Most approaches of this type do not consider the workload required for the acquisition of data by physical sensors (data sensing tasks), but only consider the load of transmitting data to remote centres and accessing data already virtualized and available via cloud. They also do not consider the actuation activities performed by IoT devices. In the following, we will analyze how the described works tackle the main requirements of IoT, as presented in Sect. 2.2, and additional features found in the solutions for IoT resource allocation based on the cloud.

Virtualization technique is traditionally adopted in cloud computing as a promising way to consolidate the requirements of heterogeneous applications onto a few numbers of computational nodes (servers), while ensuring safe co-location between competing applications. This facilitates statistical multiplexing of resources across several customers and applications, thus promoting higher resource utilization and better profits for providers [13]. Therefore, virtualization inherently addresses the IoT requirements of dealing with the heterogeneity of applications. However, with resource sharing, multiple applications now contend for the same resource pool, and it is important to develop scheduling algorithms that allocate resources in a fair and efficient manner. There has been extensive research in the cloud computing field proposing solutions for such a problem. By applying virtualization techniques on IoT, the virtualized IoT data/device is only one more type of resource for the pool: resource allocation becomes a matter of applying the mechanisms and solutions already existing for cloud systems, only adding a new dimension of the data heterogeneity and provenance. Therefore, virtualization also addresses the IoT heterogeneity in terms or devices, by abstracting them as other type of resource provided by the infrastructure. However, some authors argue that the traditional cloud computing server schedulers are not ready to provide services to IoT for different reasons. For instance, the authors in [13] mention that one of the obstacles is the lack of standardization regarding the heterogeneous devices and applications composing an IoT ecosystem. Moreover, techniques often employed in cloud systems to increase the revenue, such as resource overbooking [6–9], are not suitable for the dynamic and unpredictable arrival pattern of IoT applications. Furthermore, in a global scale IoT system, with resources being shared among heterogeneous applications, the QoS requirements to be met are also very different. A body monitoring or eHealth application is much more critical than a shopping application or a HVAC application to control the room temperature, since the former involves risks for human life. The scheduler needs to be aware of different priorities of applications when allocating the resources. Furthermore, the blending of IoT resources into the cloud introduces new resource management requirements, associated with the need to optimize not only processing, storage and I/O resources, but also sensor reading cycles, multi-sensor queries and shared access to location-dependent IoT resources [14]. Therefore, to properly meet the expectations of users, the traditional cloud computing server schedulers should be improved to efficiently schedule and allocate IoT requests by considering all their specific features, including the high heterogeneity of devices and priorities of applications.

The works presented in this section [2, 4, 10, 13] considered the aforementioned peculiarities of IoT systems, but they only address a subset of IoT requirements

Table 5.1 Comparison of approaches for cloud-only

IoT requirements		Papers			
		[2]	[4]	[10]	[13]
High scale		✓	✓	✓	✓
Heterogeneity	Devices	✓	✓	✓	✓
	Applications	✓	✓	✓	✓
Dynamic environment			✓		
Real-time processing					
Data stream processing		✓		✓	
Opportunistic interactions					
Complex QoS requirements					
Context/location-awareness			✓		
Application priority					✓
Pricing model			✓		
Mobility			✓		
Fault tolerance		✓	✓	✓	✓
Load balance/fairness		✓	✓	✓	✓

(Table 5.1). As would be expected for cloud-based solution for resource management, all the presented works take into account the heterogeneity and high scale of IoT. The work in [4] addresses the dynamicity of the IoT environments through a resource management based on the cooperation among service providers in GMCC. Since such cooperation is stimulated by a pricing mechanism and users demand, this work also contributes to the definition of the price model in IoT, at least at the level of the cloud. Their proposal is also location-aware, since this is a key feature of any approach for mobile systems.

The application priority, although an essential requirement in many IoT applications, is considered only in [13]. Since the works discussed under the cloud-only category do not explicitly consider the processing capacities of the IoT devices, they do not address the requirement of exploiting opportunistic interactions, as expected. Moreover, the delay incurred in sending all the IoT generated data to the cloud for processing makes such approaches unsuitable for real-time processing. In general, we identified that dealing with the complex QoS requirements of IoT applications is a current drawback of cloud-based solutions. On the other hand, fault tolerance and load balance are intrinsic features provided by any cloud-based approach.

5.3   IoT Cloud Approaches

The works previously discussed considered the integration of IoT devices with the cloud with the main purpose of sharing devices' resources/data via virtualization techniques. The focus of those proposals was on adapting cloud platforms to deal with the novel demands of IoT scenarios. They dealt mainly with the resource allocation challenges related to scale, heterogeneity and to the unknown number of incoming data to be processed by the cloud. In this section, we present works that move a step forward and consider the IoT devices as active entities in the resource allocation schemes.

5.3.1   Examples of IoT Cloud Approaches

The authors in [15] propose the device cloud approach, which can be seen as an application of the cloud computing infrastructure as a service (IaaS) and platform as a service (PaaS) paradigms to the IoT domain. The approach allows sharing and on demand provisioning of resources provided by the connected embedded devices. It leverages the fact that in IoT environments, multiple users can explore and utilize the available resources at the same time, while their devices become an active part of the infrastructure. With this motivation, the authors introduce the device cloud architecture which acts as a foundation for a distributed and resource-oriented middleware platform. In the proposed architecture, the infrastructure is separated in a physical space, a runtime space and a social space. The main goal is abstracting and hiding the complexity of each space, thus addressing the heterogeneity issue.

The physical space includes all collaborating physical devices, systems and networks. The nodes in this space are classified as:

- **Device Node (DN)**: refers to pure data resources (i.e. sensors);
- **Aggregation Node (AN)**: smart devices that provide compute or storage resources. ANs are the bridge between the physical and the runtime space. ANs expose all resources available in the physical space to the upper layers. ANs are the core nodes of the device cloud approach;
- **Backend Node (BN)**: nodes from this class offer data stream functionalities and aggregate management components hosted on dedicated servers.

The runtime space manages and provisions data, computation and storage resources by means of a shared resource pool. The major challenge to be tackled at this level is keeping transparency regarding heterogeneity and availability of resources, since nodes in the physical space can be temporarily unavailable, they rely on different communication and transport protocols and adopt different data formats. The main components of runtime space are: **aggregation node runtime (ANR)**, **management layer (ML)** and the **shared resource pool (SRP)**. ANR is a software component running on ANs. All ANRs together form the distributed device cloud middleware. The distribution is hidden from the other layers, which means that neither an application nor a sensor (i.e. DN) have to take care about which ANR executes or integrates them. Besides the resource integration and provisioning, ANRs provide a uniform service execution environment that abstracts the specific characteristics of the underlying device. If applications require more computation or storage resources than made available by the ANs, ANRs can also be deployed on BNs (i.e. dedicated servers). In general, ANRs provide and manage the utilization of the shared resource pool in a similar was as the PaaS paradigm. The main responsibilities of the ML are monitoring the state of the device cloud middleware, and hosting knowledge repositories used by the ANRs to adapt the system to the current needs. The ML also provides management features to cope with privacy, security and QoS issues. The SRP can be envisioned as the set of data, computation and storage resources provided by the physical space. The device cloud middleware manages and provisions these resources to users and applications. The access to resources can be realized either exclusively or in a shared way (e.g. by using sensor virtualization), but it is always managed by ANRs in conjunction with the respective ML components (e.g. access control).

The social space represents the collaborating users and their applications in the deevice cloud. Based on the runtime space, it provides an environment for executing ubiquitous applications. From the user perspective, the platform that serves his/her needs is no longer a set of statically bound physical devices, but instead a dynamic pool of shared resources.

The same group of authors of [15] later on published the paper [16] with an extended version of the device cloud framework. In this extension, the authors leverage the ad hoc collaboration among the players in an IoT system, without the need of long-term contracts to share devices and their resources. Users participate as both consumers and providers at the same time since device resources can be allocated and offered dynamically. The paper describes the refactored framework encompassing several architectural components and participants. It is organized following a domain-based approach to simplify management and provide scalability. Thus, the global pool of resources kept in the device cloud consists of several independent local pools. A domain is managed by a domain operator. Similar to an Internet service provider (ISP), the domain operator provides the basic infrastructure services required to set-up the device cloud but does not participate in the resource sharing and pooling itself. As the root authority of a domain, the domain operator is assumed to be a trusted entity. On top of the infrastructure services, the consumer operators provide the user level services required to interact with the resource pool and to manage devices. consumer operators allow users, also called consumers, to access the device cloud infrastructure, share, and allocate device resources on-demand. Multiple consumer operators may coexist within one domain. Consumers usually mandate consumer operators to manage owned devices on their behalf. The device cloud framework defines the following core architectural components:

- **Device Directory**: acts as a directory service for device resources. It provides the fundamental data model required to describe devices and represent their lifecycle (thus it keeps the resource model of the system).
- **User Directory**: provides identity and access management (IAM) services. It maintains a set of principals and allows authenticating them. Principals refer to consumers, consumers operators, ANs, etc.

- *Management Services*: represent services offered by consumer operators in order to implement the device resource provisioning process (e.g. decision policies, accounting, device locking algorithms, device access negotiation between operators).
- *Device Cloud Middleware*: it is deployed on ANs and acts as an execution environment for instances of device descriptions provided by the device directory. The device cloud middleware is the consumer's interface to its corresponding consumer operator. It acts as a bridge between allocated device resources and applications and thus performs device integration (i.e. M2M) and data aggregation or pre-processing.

Allocation of a device resource is preceded by its discovery. To decide whether a device resource is contained in the interest set, it has to be identified. Hence, a device needs to be announced to a device directory and the description of its resources made available to each domain. Each device being added to the device cloud must be registered using a unique ID (created according to one of the general IoT assumptions). The domain operator adds the device to its local pool (i.e. synchronizes its Local Directory with the Global one) and the elected consumer operator starts managing the device on behalf of the consumer. As soon as a device resource is managed by a consumer operator, it can be added to the pool and shared among the consumers. After a Consumer has discovered a device, it has to verify if the device is contained in its interest set. Therefore, the corresponding consumer operator is queried for the Device Instance and all other descriptions using the unique ID gathered during the discovery process. If the local device directory operated by the parent domain operator does not know the device resource, the global directory is queried. A synchronization protocol is used to propagate required descriptions to the local instance. The operator property of the device instance is used to determine the consumer operator managing the discovered device. Finally, a negotiation phase is initiated. If the allocation attempt succeeded, a device lock is created. This result in the creation of a device access token, which is transmitted to the consumer. The middleware instance verifies the Token and integrates the device using the M2M Platform Modules linked to the device description. Finally, the integrated device resource needs to be linked to an application. Besides defining the interest set of a consumer, the consumer profile defines a composition of aggregation platform modules for each device category present in the profile. This composition defines how the data are pre-processed (e.g. transformation to a certain format) and forwarded to applications. Therefore, each composition must be terminated with a so-called output module that is configured to transmit the data to a particular sink (e.g. a database or a monitoring application).

In [17], the same authors of [15, 17] present a use-case in the eHealth domain to emphasize the practical applicability of pooling and sharing IoT sensors and devices. The eHealth domain is a typical example of a critical IoT application, since sensors are used to monitor the vital signs of a patient, and often to trigger alarms upon the occurrence of conditions that could represent hazardous or emergency situations. Sensors are usually integrated by using gateway devices (e.g. smart phones) and the collected data is forwarded to the clinical information system of the medical facility responsible for the patient's care. In case of emergencies, several medical facilities can be involved in the treatment process. Thus, each facility needs to access the data collected from the medical sensors. Electronic health record (EHR) clouds can be used to integrate and provision the data from/to clinical information systems hosted in different medical facilities. Due to privacy constraints, two medical facilities usually have to negotiate legal contracts before they are allowed exchanging data of their patients [17]. As the authors argue in the paper, EHR clouds are mainly suitable for exchanging historical data, medication schedules and other non-real-time data about a patient. However, for real-time data such as vital signs collected by medical devices attached to a patient, the EHR approach has some drawbacks. For example, the delay introduced in the transmission to/from the cloud can yield unacceptable response times in the decision process regarding a treatment. Therefore, the authors propose that, instead of exchanging the data by linking the clinical information systems, each clinical information system is allowed the direct access to the medical devices monitoring a patient. In this context, their approach builds on sharing the devices themselves and not the data produced by them. They claim that such approach differs from sensor virtualization techniques, since the users can directly access and share the physical devices (the data sources) not only their virtual representation, via some service interface. The paper presents an IoT resource management framework, called the cooperative device cloud. Such framework is an instantiation of the device cloud approach [15, 16], now tailored for the specific context of eHealth. It allows each participant (in this case end users, public institutions, companies) to act as device consumers and device providers simultaneously, with no need of legal contracts between device consumers and providers (i.e. owners). Therefore, participants can play different roles, such as device owner, device consumer and device integrator. Usually, medical devices are exclusive resources because there is an exclusive communication link between the device and the Integrator (e.g. a smart phone or a nearby gateway) [17]. However, some devices may allow multiple systems to communicate with them. These devices are nonexclusive resources and can be shared among the participants. The sharing and provisioning of a device is based on creating device locks (i.e. access tokens). By configuring such locks, the state of the device is modified. For instance, the idle state represents a device currently not provisioned. The consumer bound state denotes a device that has received a request to be accessed. Whenever the device is integrated (in order to be provisioned in the system), it undergoes a transition to the integrator bound state, and the integrator property of the device lock is set.

The two interesting aspects of the work described in [17] for this Book are (i) the proposed vision of the physical device itself as the resource to be shared, instead of the provided data, and (ii) the need for real-time response of the system, which is an application-specific requirement to be considered as part of a solution for resource management in IoT. However, besides describing the high-level interactions of their framework to accommodate the needs of the eHealth scenario, the authors do not really describe how to meet the real-time constrains or how to negotiate the access to the available resources.

The authors in [18] present a novel framework for integrating IoT devices with cloud that improves both the scalability and the privacy-protection mechanism of the system. The proposed framework enables security solutions that protect privacy without degrading the quality of applications. At the core of the framework there is a component called *runtime adaptation engine* (RAE), implemented as an autonomous software agent to be deployed on each device and cloud participating of the IoT cloud system. The RAE plays the role of a scheduler, since it addresses the problem of choosing the entity (in the IoT cloud integrated system) to execute a given task required by the application. In the scheduling process, the framework considers the presence of different versions of processing engines, both in the smart devices and in the cloud, providing the same service but with different attributes of quality. A lighter version is deployed in a smartphone, for instance, able to process the tasks without the cost of transferring the data to the cloud over the network. However, it consumes the limited battery life of the device and provides the result with a value of accuracy not necessarily as good as that of the cloud-based processing engine, which runs on resources with higher computation capacity [18]. Therefore, to provide a good quality of user experience, and optimize system resources, the RAE performs an automatic decision process regarding the best agent to perform each task, without human intervention. For such, the RAE maintains a list of available devices and cloud, and monitors the state of their available resources. RAEs installed on different devices communicate with each other to share the respective states of the device and decide on the best workload distribution. A *logistic regression* [19] algorithm is employed to learn the most cost-effective policy for distributing tasks among devices and cloud, given the current state of resources. A cost function is defined as the weighted sum of the resource state (such as battery life), network and CPU usage. The policy obtained by running the logistic regression is enforced by a module called *device/cloud selection* module that chooses the most economical computational resources, based on the expected cost value for a given task.

In [19], the authors' main motivation is the need of dealing with the deluge of data being generated and consumed in IoT systems, requiring that the supporting frameworks provide new capabilities related to big data analysis, scalability and performance. Per the authors, the formation of local clouds of devices is a good solution to overcome these issues. The combination of local and remote resources along with the adoption of proper allocation algorithms for their management will provide the means to enable the new required features, going beyond the current state of the art. The work was developed in the context of a project that aims at building a content-centric platform distributed over a local cloud in order to provide a novel environment for IoT applications. Their focus is on applications accessing machine-to-machine (M2M) services and devices. In order to enable that M2M applications are seamlessly integrated with existing IoT heterogeneous systems, the authors presented a distributed service infrastructure called BETaaS, which provides easy deployment of applications by exposing to developers a service-oriented interface to access things regardless of the technology and the physical infrastructure they used [20]. There are multiple capabilities implemented in BETaaS, e.g. context management, QoS, security management, big data management and virtualization. The main focus of [20] is the virtualization framework of BETaaS. The virtualization capabilities are included in the BETaaS implementation for two main purposes: (1) to provide a way for deploying applications locally, and (2) to enable scalability for the platform functionalities. The platform exploits both local virtualization capabilities provided by gateways and external cloud resources provided by third parties. This is achieved by providing a set of basic images that contain pre-installed software depending on their purpose, based on a very lightweight Linux operating system. The algorithm to allocate resources minimizes fragmentation by considering the resources required by the existing VMs and the potential requirements for new instances. The priority is to exploit those resources provided by local gateways but, whenever there are no enough resources, the algorithm will try to use an external cloud. To create the local clouds, several gateways may decide to join their efforts under what the authors call a BETaaS Instance, in such a way they can share data and resources whenever necessary, in the local environment. Physical gateways and logical gateways (known as BETaaS Gateways), differ in the sense that a physical gateway could host one or more logical gateways, by using VMs. Devices (sensors, actuators, etc.) can connect to existing gateways (physical or virtual) in order to produce data that will be consumed by applications.

In order to predict the usage of resources before taking a resource allocation decision, a double exponential smoothing (also known as Holt's Linear method [21]) was applied for determining the amount of storage, CPU and memory usage. If the local deployment is selected as the best option, there will be a process for determining the most adequate gateway for hosting the new VM. In case, the remote deployment is selected, there will be a check of the remote cloud conditions and availability (the Internet connection might be down). Whenever there is an issue and the local deployment is an available option, it will be then performed. The virtualization feature in local clouds is managed by BETaaS Platform. The core architecture (deployed in each BETaaS Gateway) is divided in three layers. The **service layer is** the top layer providing applications with APIs to for their installation and management. The **Things as a Service (TaaS) Layer** is in charge of the management of resources, by providing *things* as services and controlling their allocation to applications. The **Adaptation Laye**r is the closest to the physical world, acting as a bridge between the things and the BETaaS Platform. While the resources manager is in charge of the resources allocation, the VM Manager is the component responsible for managing the lifecycle of the VM resources. Both are part of the **TaaS** layer and interact with other components such as the big data manager (which provides functionalities to the Service and TaaS layers), the service manager (located in the Service layer only) and the dependability manager (also, in the Service layer).

Since the architecture has been designed to work in a distributed way, gateways located in the same instance share information about their resources availability and can request resources from others. Therefore, the TaaS Resources Manager is able to determine the best deployment strategy. The VM Manager interacts with a hypervisor and controls the creation, deletion and other managing tasks related to the VMs (i.e. monitoring), both locally and remotely. It is based on the usage of predefined images (called VM templates or flavours), available in the instance gateways and in a BETaaS public server. While the service manager and the big data manager are responsible for requesting resources to the TaaS resources manager for deploying an application or providing resources for data analytics, the dependability manager supports the operation of the platform, detecting and solving availability issues in components and VMs. The instance manager component controls the BETaaS instances formation. It manages the 'local clouds', controlling the join procedure for new gateways and the dismiss procedure of old ones for reasons of problematic or malicious behaviour.

Another work that also exploits the benefits of creating local clouds is described in [22]. Such work was developed in the context of an interesting class of systems that can compose an IoT ecosystem, namely the vehicular networks. In this case, the connected things are the vehicles themselves, instrumented by sensors able to produce several types of environmental data. In [22] the authors discuss resource management issues for cloud-based vehicular networks. Instead of focusing on the resource allocation in wireless communication, the authors proposed an interesting approach in which the participating vehicles are integrated to compose a local cloud aiming at sharing resources. The authors argue that the vision of all vehicles connected, either in the context of smart road applications [23], intelligent transport system (ITS), or to build a vehicular ad hoc network [24] poses a significant challenge to the collection, storage and processing of large amounts of data. To address this challenge, they propose to integrate cloud computing into vehicular networks so that the vehicles can share computation, storage and bandwidth resources. Then, the authors investigate cloud resource allocation and virtual machine migration for effective resource management in this cloud-based vehicular network. A hierarchical cloud architecture for vehicular networks is proposed and a game-theoretical approach is presented to optimally allocate cloud resources.

By adopting a different approach, the authors in [25] propose a middleware system, named service-oriented composer for orchestrating real-time proximity-based industrial Internet of Things (SCORPII). The proposed middleware provides an efficient task allocation strategy in an architecture composed of mobile IoT devices and utility cloud services. The authors tackle the problem of resource allocation considering that certain tasks of mobile applications can be offloaded to utility cloud services to reduce resource usage at the mobile devices. The middleware utilizes dynamic elastic cloud computing and workflow automation to optimize the task allocation among mobile devices and cloud services based on the resource availability and cost-performance index model.

SCORPII architecture encompasses a mobile host side (ScoMH) and utility cloud side (ScoUC). The ScoMH is the main controller of the entire middleware and consists of a set of components as following. A set of communication protocols enable short range networked resource discovery and interaction (Bluetooth,

ZigBee, etc.). A web service mediator allows ScoMH to interact with global net-worked services. A cloud service mediator dynamically configures and launches virtual machine instances and sets up the needed components to setup the ScoUC. The normalized message routing control component processes messages to meet the required format for the receivers of the message. The Request Handling (RHUC) component acts as message broker receiving request messages from other appli-cations and forwards them to corresponding components through the normalized message routing control component. The workflow manager manages, monitors and executes workflows. The resource state management component is responsible for monitoring resource usage, such as CPU usage, network bandwidth usage, utility service usage, etc. The service pool is in charge of managing service description of internal services, utility cloud services and services provided by external service providers. Functional components encompasses utility components such as semantic metadata matchmaking component, message parsing and calculation component, for calculating the cost performance index (CPI) value. Finally, ScoMH has components to ensure trustworthy, secure and QoS.

The cloud side of the architecture, ScoUC, is launched and terminated on-demand where instances of services can be stored as a snapshot in cloud storage to reduce the need of uploading files directly from mobile host. The authors claim that the main advantage of such a design is to fully reach the utility cloud service concept of pay-per-use. The ScoUC has the following components. The workflow engine (WEUC) oversees handling a workflow execution received from the ScoMH. The App Manager is in charge of matching available Web application to tasks according to the needs of the workflow engine. The App Manager also handles Web applications deployment to prepare them to be used by the WEUC. The RHUC oversees analyzing and processing the payload of request messages in order to perform corresponding actions. The communication manager handles network communication between ScoUC and ScoMH, and also between ScoUC and external entities.

The resource allocation in SCORPII is done through a *cost performance index-*based scheme. Such a scheme defines a **Cost element set** E as a finite set where each element of E is a tuple containing a *unique identification* and a *cost value* (CPU usage, RAM, bandwidth, cost of cloud service, etc.). An **abstract workflow model** describes the structure of a process in high abstraction level. Each request received by SCORPII, specified as an abstract workflow, triggers a corresponding workflow execution process (set of parallel and sequence tasks). **A task type** *tType* denotes a type of node that represents the main task of an abstract workflow and it is defined as a 3-tuple containing the identification of *tType* (*ID*); the input message type (*IN*) and the output message type (*OUT*) of *tType*. A *tType* node can be replaced by another *tType* node or by another workflow as long as the substitution matches the *IN* and the *OUT* of the original *tType* node. A task of to be accom-plished is called a **work item** that is executed by a **resource**. A resource in the context of SCORPII model is a localhost component or a Web application that has been deployed in the cloud. When a resource is executing a work item, it is called an **activity**.

Additionally, the authors define the term **approach** to denote a tuple encompassing an Abstract workflow model, a mapping of nodes to activities, a mapping of activities to resources, a mapping of activities to cost elements and a mapping of activities to time span. An approach can consist of one or multiple activities (individual workflow). A *tType* node in an abstract workflow model can be accomplished by different approaches as long as the approach satisfies the *IN* and the *OUT* of the *tType* node. The *approach* of a *tType* node can change dynamically at runtime. However, the activities in an *approach* cannot change after the *approach* is chosen since the mapping elements of the *approach* have already defined its whole configuration (mapping elements). An activity can be performed by a predefined *approach* or it can be performed by a dynamic defined *approach* at runtime. Based on the dependence among the activities of an approach, a few routes can be discovered. Each route may consume different time-span depending on the activities involved. Since the shortest time-span is not enough to define the most efficient resource allocation, SCORPII introduces the CPI scheme to optimize the approach selection. Such a scheme combines fuzzy set and the weight of context [26]. The reason they use fuzzy set is to compare the performance and cost between approaches instead of using static values. A formula is presented to generate the ranking value for *approaches* in which the lower time span the *approach* has, the higher ranking value it has. Following, they compute the normalized fuzzy number of the ranking value. They also consider the importance weight of each cost element, since a cost element may be different for different users. For instance, when the device battery life is low, the user may consider that saving the battery life of his/her mobile device is more important than the money cost of using cloud services. In this case, the weight of the battery life cost element will be higher than the weight of the bandwidth cost of the cloud service.

A comprehensive solution for resource management that allow IoT services to fully leverage the capabilities of the cloud infrastructures is proposed by the OpenIoT project [27]. The authors in [28] argue that most of the current researches that integrate cloud and IoT focus on streaming sensor data into the cloud to allow IoT applications to take advantage of the elasticity and the storage capacity of the cloud. However, this integration is not properly designed to optimize the usage of both IoT and cloud resources in an integrated cloud/IoT environment. Moreover, they claim that an effective resource management mechanism requires a well-defined semantics in terms of sensor metadata to not only to identify which sensors and/or data are required in the scope of specific IoT applications but also to allow the dynamic selection of data streams and their data elements. The reason behind this lies in the fact that the optimization strategies need to access information about the metadata of the sensors and their data (e.g. location, orientation, timestamps, measurement units, reliability, accuracy, cost, data frequency) and rich described metadata are needed to build sophisticated and efficient resource management schemes. In this context, the OpenIoT framework introduces an architecture for IoT/cloud convergence, which tackles the aforementioned limitations of state-of-the-art infrastructures. The novel characteristics are the integration of rich metadata to describe sensors and the data streams and the exploitation of such feature to support scheduling of IoT services in the cloud. The richness of the metadata description is achieved by using semantic web technologies and standards, including standardized ontologies for describing internet-connected objects and their data streams. On top of this semantic layer a two-level resource allocation scheme is built, where resource reservations are supported at both the cloud infrastructure level (global scheduler) and individual sensor deployments level (local scheduler).

The Global Scheduler is in charge of processing requests for IoT services deployment ensuring their proper access to their required resources (such as data streams). To this end, the global scheduler parses and analyses the service request to discover and select the sensors (resources) that can contribute to its fulfilment, while also performing the relevant reservations of resources. The scheduler keeps track of and controls the lifecycle of IoT services and manages all the metadata of the IoT services, including: (1) the input and output parameters of the IoT service, (2) the sensors used to provide the service, and (3) the service execution parameters, such as the data delivery mode (intervals in which the service shall be repeated), and other resources used by the service. The local scheduler is executed at the level of the sensor middleware and ensures the optimized access to the resources managed by GSN nodes (see Sect. 5.3.1). Therefore, while the global scheduler manages the access to the resources residing in the cloud, the local scheduler manages the access and use of the data streams at the lower level of the sensor middleware layer (such a middleware can be positioned as residing in a fog tier).

Since the OpenIoT scheduler enables the availability and provision of accurate information about sensors and their generated data requested by each service, a variety of resource management and optimization algorithms can be implemented at the scheduler component of the OpenIoT. Moreover, the two-level scheduling scheme facilitates resource optimization at the sensor data-acquisition level (at the fog). The scheduler components maintain information that can be used to optimize the use of the infrastructure through aggregate operations, such as the aggregation of queries within the cloud. Furthermore, in-network processing and data management techniques can be implemented to optimize processing times and/or reduce the required access to the WSN. In order to explore such a potential, the current OpenIoT framework implement two resource optimization schemes [28]. The first scheme is an in-network process that occurs at the X-GSN node level and ensures no unnecessary data will be streamed from the sensors to the cloud. Therefore, this scheme provides saving in terms of bandwidth and costs associated with cloud access. This scheme relies on a periodic timed (i.e. polling) task that runs on the X-GSN module and queries the LSM/W3C SSN repository to determine which sensors are necessary to run IoT services. Then, the task compares the result of the query with the list of sensors that are currently active on the X-GSN sensor middleware module. The sensors that are needed by an IoT service but are not active in the X-GSN are activated while the sensors that are active but not needed are deactivated. The second scheme is based on caching of SPARQL queries/requests [29]. Such a scheme is crucial for any semantic-based resource management framework. A notable drawback of the use of triple stores is their low performance compared to other conventional repositories such as relational databases. The caching solution employs a proxy layer that intercepts all SPARQL queries and checks whether the result has already been cached. If the response to the query is cached, that data is sent to the client directly through the cache without accessing the SPARQL data store. On the other hand, the query is forwarded to the SPARQL engine and the result is cached at the proxy layer. The caching of SPARQL queries reduce network traffic, enhance the availability of data to the users, and reduce the cost of potentially expensive cloud-access operations.

Some works tackle to resource allocation problem from the point of view of software-defined networking (SDN) paradigm. The paper [30] identifies the components of an IoT ecosystem as being organized into four layers. The first layer (Layer 1) is the sensing layer, consisting in sensors, RFIDs, and wireless sensor networks (WSN). Information produced by this layer is collected by the aggregation layer (Layer 2). Examples of aggregator elements are the sink nodes in WSN, responsible for gathering sensor generated data and uploading them to the Internet. Smartphones or specialized gateways can also play this role. Aggregators either directly process the data or send them to processing nodes located at Layer 3. After data is processed, it can be uploaded to the cloud via an Internet connection (Layer 4). Once in the cloud, data can be made available for utilization by a large number of users and applications. Heterogeneity is present in the four layers and the SDN paradigm is employed in all of them to enable centralized network management, thus allowing efficient optimization and configuration. Regarding the management of the sensing layer, the SDN controller can be implemented at the sink node or aggregator points. The centralized position of the controller makes it suitable for making optimal decisions about the resource allocation for the system. Controllers can, for instance, optimize the logical topology by configuring the sleep/active cycles of the sensors. The global, holistic view of the controller allows it to choose the most energy-efficient set of nodes in every scheduling cycle. In a higher layer, for dealing with the end-to-end resource management, the SDN controller is logically centralized between all network entities, e.g. service providers, backbone and radio access networks (RAN). The controller communicates with the operators to generate and implement policies for resource sharing according to the network load and other conditions. Although the authors do not present a specific solution or algorithm to perform the resource allocation, the proposed architecture allows joint optimization of RANs and backbone networks, thus facilitating achieving a holistic resource management and improving the QoS delivered to final users.

In [31] the authors present the concept of *cloud-based software-defined wireless networking (SDWN)*. SDWN extends the traditional SDN architecture to encompass mobile cloud computing networks. The key idea is to utilize data centres for complex network management by leveraging their geographical distribution along with the cloud virtualization features, and to exploit SDN capabilities of traceable traffic flows and centralized management, in order to optimize the resource utilization. Since cloud resources in data centres are geographically distributed over a WAN, there is a need of multiple CSPs to meet the user/application needs. Moreover, in cloud-based SDWNs, CSPs are allowed to share resources in order to enhance their capability. Upon receiving an application request, whenever a data centre has enough resources to run the application by accommodating all its needs, CSP can directly allocate local resources to it. Otherwise, instead of potentially refusing new applications when it has fewer resources, CSP can rent resources from either remote or local CSPs. In the paper [31], a resource allocation and sharing scheme for CSPs in SDWN is proposed, and the authors discuss the competition and cooperation between CSPs. The resource configurations among CSPs are classified into local and remote. In remote resource sharing, users are allowed to access remote CSPs and execute their applications on remote devices. CSPs consider communication cost, latency constraints, and resource utilization. In the Local approach, the resource sharing strategy is complicated by the economic agreements between different CSPs. CSPs that have sufficient resources place their resources into a resource pool and obtain profit from leasing their resources to other CSPs. On the other hand, CSPs with resources that are already highly utilized may opt for achieving more available resources by trading in the local cloud resource market. Trading can be carried on by competition (CSPs compete with each other and act in a selfish way) and cooperation (CSPs cooperate with each other and maximize the global benefits).

The ultimate goal of CSPs in cloud-based SDWNs is to maximize their own revenues while delivering high QoS. Revenue can be obtained from service provision. Thus, CSPs have higher resource utilization and obtain more revenue if they provide more services. However, CSPs whose resources are already highly utilized will potentially obtain a lower QoS since fewer resources are available for new users. CSPs aim to maximize their utility, which is used to evaluate their performance (e.g. in terms of revenue and QoS). Therefore, the resource sharing behaviour, concretized as resource trading activity among CSPs is formulated as a Nash bargaining game. CSPs in the game will negotiate price for better utility [31]. In the cloud resource market, CSPs can be buyers or sellers. Sellers form a resource pool and sell resources with an agreed price while buyers compete for the limited resources. Sellers are the CSPs with low resource utilization who place unoccupied resources in the resource pool for short-term leasing. Buyers are the CSPs who can rent the resources from the resource pool. Results of the comparison between the cooperation and the competition policies show that the former can obtain more revenue for CSPs than the later. Besides, the cooperation policy can achieve two goals that are very useful for a RMS: flexible resource management, thus accommodating the dynamic environment, and demand-driven resource distribution.

In [32] the authors go a step beyond the collaboration between IoT and cloud systems and investigate resource management in the context of IoT cloud federations. The focus of the paper is to present a flexible IoT Cloud federation energy management strategy to optimize the allocation of geographically localized smart sensors.

The authors in [32] consider an IoT cloud provider as a company that offers sensing and actuating services to other companies, entities or people. It provides services by abstracting, virtualizing and managing computational resources according to specific service-level agreements (SLAs). IoT cloud providers are able to make contracts both with public and private entities and/or users/customers. They are particularly useful for users and small businesses to serve as outsourcing target, when the users of the larger cloud providers request some special kind of service. In this scenario, a cloud provider must define the service level to fulfil its SLA requirements. In a federated IoT cloud environment, a cloud broker, instead, is a third-party subject, generally a company, that acts as an intermediary between IoT cloud providers that want to establish federation partnerships. Hence, the brokerage is a key element, allowing an IoT cloud provider (called a cloud initiator in the paper) to select one or more external providers (denoted as target clouds) to establish a federation relationship.

Each IoT cloud holds several sensor nodes, each one running multiple virtual sensors deployed in Linux OS environments called containers. A lightweight virtualization technology for IoT devices, called linux container virtualization (LCV), allows containers to wrap up pieces of software to be run. If compared to VMs, containers have a different architectural approach so that they are much more portable and efficient. Containerization techniques have been exploited in the context of edge computing, further discussed in Sect. 5.5. Moreover, each federated IoT cloud can manage different sub-environments which can include both local virtual sensors and virtual sensors deployed in other federated IoT clouds. IoT cloud providers and broker actions in such a federated environment should be finalized to carry out an efficient energy management of the whole ecosystem [32]. Therefore, an IoT cloud provider can ask for external resources (e.g. virtual sensors and actuators) to other providers for multiple reasons including resource enlargement, resource optimization, costs reduction, security, QoS, deployment of distributed services, fault tolerance, energy efficiency (to reduce energy costs and/or for energy sustainability purposes) and so on. This is made possible using the container virtualization on IoT devices that allows migrating resources or services (virtual sensors and actuators) from an IoT cloud to another. In this paper, the authors focus on energy sustainability in IoT cloud federation. Their approach allows the federated ecosystem to implement specific policies to dynamically select the best destination where to allocate/migrate virtual sensors and actuators. They leverage the dynamic deployment of containers to run services with good performances and reduced start up time [33]. Although this means to assume that costs for the hosting service are strongly related to the availability and the effective energy consumption at the specific cloud sensor node, their strategy is focused on improving energy sustainability for the whole federated cloud ecosystem, and they succeed in achieving such a goal.

In their proposed strategy to enforce energy sustainability in a federated IoT cloud environment [32], an IoT cloud provider that receives a request from a user, or that identifies an unsustainable IoT device running a virtual sensor in its infrastructure, contacts the broker to get an energy sustainable hosting to which migrate its virtual sensor. The monitored environment is divided in several sub-environments where each one represents the minimum coverage area for measurement (sensing coverage), determined on the basis of each specific use-case. A broker that receives a request from an IoT cloud provider identifies the use-case in terms of phenomena, accuracy in the size of the sub-environment, and activities. Therefore, it starts looking for external providers belonging to the federation considering the requirements of the use-case, to determine several possible available IoT clouds. At the next step, the IoT cloud requesting the hosting service receives from the broker an input data set including the energy parameters of external federated clouds. This data set is mainly expressed in terms of the power consumption requested to run the virtual sensor. Thus, the IoT cloud runs an algorithm to determine in which federated IoT cloud the virtual sensor should be deployed. For purposes of protecting the privacy of the involved parties, since the requesting IoT cloud does not desire to expose its businesses, it sends to the broker a data stream which contains only values to solve the request.

5.3.2   Discussion

Unlike approaches that consider the IoT devices as passive data sources and delegate all work to the cloud, the proposals presented in this section leverage the collaborative processing between IoT devices and cloud. Such collaboration takes advantage of the devices computing capacity, considering such nodes as active players in the resource provision process. As showed in [18], among the benefits of such approaches, by exploiting the resources available at millions of smart mobile devices, user's requests can be met more quickly, and the cost of cloud management can be significantly reduced. Moreover, besides the benefits related to cost and performance, issues related to user privacy, one of the controversial limitations of cloud usage in the IoT context, can be resolved. Personal data can be processed within a device or the obfuscated version of such data can be sent to the cloud [18]. One key drawback of cloud only approaches that can be overcome when considering the Things layer as active part of the RM is achieving real-time data delivery. Clouds are mainly suitable for exchanging historical data due to the delay introduced in the transmission to/from the cloud, which can yield unacceptable response times in the critical process such as eHealth applications. In this context, the IoT cloud approach provides means to build flexible sharing models such as the one described in [18] where sharing occurs at the device level and not only on the data produced by them.

Table presents the comparison of the IoT cloud approaches based on the IoT requirements tackled by them. Like the works in the cloud-only Section, all the works presented in this section propose RM solutions that take into account the high scale of IoT data as well as the heterogeneity of devices and applications. The dynamicity of the IoT environment is addressed by [15–18, 20] through mechanisms that monitor the context of the environment and adapt the system state accordingly. Unlike one would expect in works that considers the IoT devices on the RM scheme, key requirements for managing IoT resources, such as mobility, real-time and data stream processing are addressed by only few works. Data stream processing is addressed in [15, 28, 32]; mobility in [17, 22, 25, 30, 31]; and

Table 5.2 Comparison of approaches for IoT cloud

IoT requirements		Papers										
		[15]	[16]	[17]	[18]	[20]	[22]	[25]	[32]	[28]	[30]	[31]
High scale		✓	✓	✓	✓	✓	✓	✓	✓	✓	✓	✓
Heterogeneity	Devices	✓	✓	✓	✓	✓	✓	✓	✓	✓	✓	✓
	Applications	✓	✓	✓	✓	✓	✓	✓	✓	✓	✓	✓
Data stream processing		✓							✓	✓		
Dynamic environment		✓	✓	✓	✓	✓						
Pricing model												✓
Complex QoS requirements					✓	✓		✓	✓	✓	✓	✓
Context/location-awareness				✓		✓	✓	✓	✓	✓		
Mobility				✓			✓	✓			✓	✓
Fault tolerance						✓			✓			
Application priority												
Opportunistic interactions		✓	✓	✓								
Load balance/fairness						✓	✓		✓			
Real-time processing				✓				✓				

real-time processing is addressed by two works: [17, 25]. The work in [31] can be considered addressing price modelling since the cooperation among the components of the system is stimulated by a pricing mechanism and users demand. Fault tolerance is another requirement neglected by most of the work, only [20] and [32] explicitly take into consideration some level of fault tolerance in their solutions. Opportunistic interactions are another requirement investigated by few works [15–17] (Table 5.2).

5.4   IoT Only Approaches

In this section, we will discuss proposals for resource allocation that consider only the entities at the Things tier as the major players, without relying on powerful external devices as the cloud computers. Such proposals inherit from and have similarities with the field of wireless sensor networks (WSN) [34]. There is a vast literature addressing resource allocation and task scheduling in the specific context of WSN. In these works, applications are broken down into tasks and such tasks are allocated to the sensor nodes. The decision on the task allocation can be performed centrally, with algorithms running on the gateway nodes and using global knowledge of the network status. More rarely, such decision can be carried out in a fully or partially distributed manner, with nodes working together based upon their local knowledge of their own state and the state of their neighbouring nodes. In any case, the main goal in resource allocation decisions for WSN is always minimizing the energy consumption of the network devices. Almost always, the satisfaction of such a requirement, per which the network lifetime should be maximized, must be balanced with meeting application-specific QoS, such as delay, data accuracy and sensing coverage. Given that there are multiple requirements, sometimes conflicting, to be tackled, the task allocation problem is often formalized as a multi-objective optimization problem, solved by using heuristic algorithms [35–38] or a metaheuristic, as for instance genetic algorithms [39] or swarm intelligence [40]. Works focused only on the WSN field are not the target of this Book. However, one could argue that existing approaches from this field can be applied directly on IoT to solve the resource allocation problem. As we will see from the works described as follows, there are additional challenges posed by the key requirements of IoT systems. In the following, we classify the proposals to be discussed in two categories: the first encompasses works that directly inherits from the WSN field, and the second includes works specifically tailored for IoT, from their inception.

5.4.1 WSN-Based Approaches

One approach widely adopted to integrate WSNs into IoT ecosystems is the virtualization of these networks and their devices. The topic of virtualization has been discussed previously in this book. No doubt, to accommodate the IoT requirements, there is a clear need of investigating novel solutions departing from traditional application-specific WSNs towards general purposes WSNs that allow the smart reuse of artefacts and promote resource sharing among multiple applications. In [41], the authors focus on the virtualization of WSN within the broader IoT field and address the resource allocation problem in this context. They consider WSNs as the underpinning infrastructures upon which large-scale cyber-physical systems are built, and then propose a virtualization engine for general purpose WSNs. They do not present a sophisticated model for the creation of virtual sensor nodes, but instead, they tackle the issue of sharing the available resources provided by the nodes among multiple applications. By decoupling the sensing and communication infrastructure from specific target applications, they promote the view of the WSN as a pool of resources that must be efficiently allocated to the applications to be deployed on the infrastructure. The authors claim that a key differential between their proposal and others in this context is that, instead of providing 'practical' building blocks to build virtual sensor networks, they focus on the 'intelligence' to properly and efficiently allocate physical resources to virtual applications, which can be modelled as a general resource allocation problem. They present a mathematical programming framework to optimally allocate shared physical resources to the concurrent applications, while accounting for the network-and hardware-specific constraints (such as processing, storage, available bandwidth, and limited communication range) besides considering the specific application requirements. They initially prove that the addressed problem of multi-application deployment in a set of resource-constrained WSN nodes is NP-complete. The reference problem used in the proof is the multiple knapsack, a mixed-integer linear programming (MILP) problem which is known to be NP-complete. The presented proof is based on specifying the additional restrictions to be added to the application deployment problem so that the resulting restricted problem will be identical to the multiple knapsack problems. As an NP-complete problem, the time required to solve the resource allocation/application deployment increases very quickly as the size of the problem grows and therefore it may be not scalable, as the authors demonstrate in the paper. Consequently, they propose a heuristic iterative algorithm to obtain sub-optimal solutions to the problem in reduced computation time. The proposed algorithm follows a classical approach based on the linear programming (LP) relaxation of the original MILP problem [42]. In short, the algorithm is based on the iterative resolution of simplified relaxed LP problems, by increasingly adding new constrains in each iteration.

In the problem formulation, the authors consider a set of sensor nodes and a set of applications to be deployed in the target geographic area. They also consider a set of test points which are physical locations where sensing variables required by the applications must be measured. Such test points are part of the application requirements, since each application tasks the WSN to sense a given set of test points. Formally, an application has to be deployed in a subset of nodes from the complete set of WSN nodes such that all the required test points are covered. They consider that a test point is covered by a sensor node if it is within its sensing range. A necessary condition for an application to be successfully deployed is that all the test points in its target set are properly sensed. Each application is further characterized by a requirement vector which specifies the generated data rate (bit/s), memory (bits) and processing load (MIPS) consumed by the application when it is deployed on a sensor node. Such vector can be regarded as the resources necessary to execute the workload generated by the application in the network. Each sensor node composing the WSN is characterized by a resource vector which specifies its available bandwidth, storage capabilities, processing power and energy supply. The wireless communication model adopted in the work considers the use of a protocol with power control as described in [43] and assumes that all the nodes under the interference range of a sensor node share the same transmission channel, thus the transmission time must be divided between them.

The main goal of the specified problem of application assignment for virtual sensor networks is to maximize the weighted number of deployed applications subject to coverage constraints (the set of test points of each application must be sensed) and application requirements (each application should be assigned enough bandwidth, and processing and storage resources to operate successfully) [41]. They assume a static routing strategy, in which there are predefined routes from each sensor node to a sink. Finally, they define a preference vector encompassing all the applications to be deployed. The elements of this vector represent the revenue for the network provider for having each application successfully deployed in the network. The specified objective function aims at maximizing the overall revenue out of the application deployment process while minimizing the cost related to the activating sensor nodes. Constraints on coverage, bandwidth and resources available in the sensors are considered in the problem formulation. Energy constraints are also included to ensure that the application deployment pattern guarantees a minimum lifetime for the virtual sensor network.

The authors in [44] also address the need to adapt traditional WSNs to integrate them in an IoT system, but adopt a different view, not explicitly based on the use of virtualization. They claim that "The vision of a state-of-the-art Internet of Things (IoT) is less realizable than what we, as researchers and developers, envisioned". They argue that only by exploring legacy technologies and trying to force them to adapt to the complex IoT scenario is not sufficient. Instead, "… a true leap to the IoT requires a grounded, yet radical, shift in paradigms [44]". In this context, and considering WSNs as major enabling resources for IoT, their work focuses on the challenges to be addressed to adapt the operation of such networks to be used in the envisioned IoT ecosystem. They present a novel paradigm in which WSNs are built as generic platforms of dynamically assigned resources for running concurrently multiple applications. In their proposal, nodes from multiple WSNs are considered as resource providers, to be shared by the applications. By assigning measurable attributes to these shared resources, it is possible to increase their utilization and better exploit the operational capacity of multiple WSN platforms. Their proposal is presented in three phases, namely: (1) resource abstraction and representation, (2) application representation as a finite set of functional requirements over these resources and (3) an optimal mapping approach to assign applications (their functionalities) to the available resources across existing WSNs [44]. An interesting aspect of their work regards the proposed abstraction for resources. In their definition of WSN resources, they encompass IoT components that are only temporarily passing by the coverage area of the WSN. For instance, smartphones, municipal antennas, smart things endowed with different technologies of access networks and other IoT devices, are all included in the pool of resources make available by the integrated system. In this sense, besides the resources provided by a set of well-defined WSN nodes, their approach exploits the opportunistic interactions enabled by the context-dependent presence of smart things. This is an important requirement to build truly integrated IoT systems, which calls, on one hand, for designing WSN nodes able to be dynamically reprogramed instead of following pre-configured operations, and on the other hand, for allowing the seamless integration of the available resources from the WSN and IoT devices. A premise considered in the work to enable such scenario regards the recent advancements in connectivity across different access networks, and the recent advancement in vertical handoffs that leverage resource management when enforced. Therefore, they assume that interconnectivity between different wireless communication technologies used by the devices is assured by the network operators.

Another requirement to enable their envisioned integrated view of multiple WSNs and other IoT resources, as well as to provide the fully utilization of such resources is adopting a clear and rigorous representation. In a position paper [45] the same authors have first described their proposed representation of resources as being composed of six core attributes, encompassing resources, their availability and usability. Details about that aspect of the proposal are discussed in Chap. 3.

Besides clearly specifying the resources to be shared, the authors define an application as a finite set of functional requirements, to be met by the existing resources and over a given time duration. Therefore, a mapping needs to be established between the available resources and the application's requirements. Given the dynamic and opportunistic nature of the integrated IoT system, they consider a best effort approach for such a mapping, with two possible outcomes: (i) the application requirements could be met, hence optimal assignment of tasks to resources need to take place, or (ii) the current resources cannot meet the application's demands, hence new resources need to be introduced or requirements relaxed [44]. The ultimate goal of the mapping function is to increase the overall network utility, which denotes the combined satisfaction degree of the multiple applications running in the system. Network utility (NU) is formally defined as "an aggregated indicator of the degree by which multiple applications are served, such that resource utilization is maximized across platforms while global network constraints are maintained" [44]. Thus, they identify maximizing the network utility as an optimization problem and adopt aLP formulation to solve the mapping problem. The formalized problem has two sets of constraints: (i) network level constraints such as lifetime, and threshold of allowed loads on certain (mostly pivotal) nodes/resources and (ii) application level constraints. The notion of satisfiability is defined in the paper as the ratio of functional requirements of a given application that are met. For example, if an application requires images taken at ten locations, and only eight of them are possible, then its satisfiability is 80%. Thus, network utility is the aggregation of the satisfiability of all applications it serves.

The paper [46] presents the resource allocation in heterogeneous sensor networks (SACHSEN) algorithm as a new resource allocation heuristic to address the challenges faced by running multiple applications onto heterogeneous WSNs. Although they do not focus specifically on the context IoT, the authors address the challenge mentioned earlier, of adapting WSN to the requirements of this environment, particularly about running multiple applications with different requirements. SACHSEN is the core of a resource allocation component of the MARINE service-oriented WSN middleware [47]. SACHSEN effectively exploits the heterogeneity and application diversity aiming to maximize the system lifetime while meeting minimum performance requirements of applications. In comparison with most resource allocation approaches in WSN, that only consider a single application at a time, SACHSEN is developed to allocate applications (including simultaneous arrivals) to sensor nodes based on the application utility which is decided by selected QoS requirements, as well as fully exploiting the system heterogeneity.

The proposal assumes a heterogeneous system encompassing several WSNs, each one with a different number (and types) of sensor nodes. Their view of a WSN system complies with our view of an IoT system covering several heterogeneous entities including WSNs. These WSNs are loosely connected by a communication network and independently managed and accessed by different sink nodes. The system architecture has three major elements, namely a web server, sink nodes and sensor nodes and it is organized in a hierarchical manner. The web server acts as a gateway node responsible for handling dynamic arrivals of application, decomposing an application into tasks, and for deciding how to dispatch the incoming tasks to WSNs based on predefined criteria and updated information about the participant WSNs. Therefore, it plays the role of a global scheduler in the system, making the initial decisions about the task partitioning based on a global view of the system components. The authors define task as the units of execution that compose an application submitted by users. User submitted applications often have specific QoS requirements that must be met by the integrated system. The QoS requirements in WSNs can be specified from two perspectives, application QoS and network QoS. In [46], the authors use data accuracy (application QoS) and system lifetime (network QoS) as the selected metrics to calculate application utility since they are strongly related to the entire system performance. The rationale behind SACHSEN is that in the resource allocation process, one can exploit the fact that different applications may share the same sensing data provided that the data they are interested in have common characteristics in time and space, and similar QoS requirements. In such a case, a new application will not necessarily incur an increase of the usage of the WSN resources. The goal of the task allocation is to find out a mapping for each application on a set of sensor nodes to maximize the heterogeneous WSN system lifetime subject to application requirements. Thus, the system lifetime of the heterogeneous WSN system is determined by the minimum network lifetime of a WSN in the system, which is also the minimum sensor lifetime in that WSN. They defined a cost function that considers energy consumption and data accuracy for each application arriving in the system. Since the task allocation problem is shown to be an NP-hard problem, thus a heuristic algorithm is employed to solve this problem in polynomial time.

SACHSEN operation starts with a locality-aware service discovery. When a new application arrives, the resource manager middleware component, installed on the web server, analyses the composition of the application. Several important pieces of information that help generating a first task-sensor assignment are extracted from this service analysis process, including the number of tasks, requested service type of each task and the geographical location of interest. In traditional Web services, the incoming task (user-request) can be randomly distributed to a service provider which can provide the corresponding service. However, due to the limitation of sensor hardware, each sensor node is constrained by its sensing range and only the physical phenomenon within that range can be detected. Thus, sensor nodes are filtered, by considering the locations of available sensor nodes, their sensing ranges and the location of requested task, and the filtered sensor nodes are all put into a candidate sensor list, to be used as input for the proposed heuristic algorithm.

5.4.2   IoT Approaches

The authors in [48] address the resource allocation problem in IoT from a QoS-centric perspective. They argue that traditional QoS attributes, such as throughput, delay or jitter, are not enough in the IoT context, which requires further requirements as data accuracy, the required network and energy resources, sensing coverage, among others. Even parameters that are well defined in other contexts are somehow poorly understood in the emergent IoT paradigm. For instance, it is still difficult to define the 'quality' of the services in IoT. The concept of 'network lifetime', which has several well-known definitions in WSN, is still not properly defined in IoT with all the heterogeneous entities involved. A novel QoS model for service-oriented IoT is thus, necessary. Such model should allow the integrated handling of the information accuracy, coverage, energy consumption, the cost of a network deployment, along with traditional QoS attributes. Moreover, solutions for QoS provisioning in IoT must be able to balance the network availability with the quality of the delivered information. Therefore, the authors propose a three-layer QoS model for service-oriented IoT to tackle these issues. In the proposed model, QoS provisioning in IoT is investigated in terms of a top-down decision-making process encompassing the application layer, the network layer and the sensing layer. A QoS analysis framework is proposed to evaluate services, networks and sensing devices, which is able to guide the optimization of QoS attributes [48]. Besides the QoS model and framework, optimization algorithms for the three layers are provided in the paper.

In their proposal, the authors call IoT edge nodes the devices at the sensing layer. These IoT edge nodes are, for instance, RFID tags or sensor nodes, and are responsible for collecting information on the physical environment and transmitting it over the network layer to the service users/providers. Resources are reserved for services in a proactive way. In IoT, services can be provided over multiple technologies of access networks. The authors claim that, in order to minimize the entire cost of a service, it is necessary to optimizing the quality at all layers, including the application, network services and end-node performance.

Their three-layered QoS-centric decision-making process is as follows:

- *Application layer*: At this layer, an application is selected to establish a connection in the IoT ecosystem, and the decisions are made by the user and by a module called *QoS scheduling engine*. In general, the *QoS module* must allocate network resources to services that are selected in the application layer. In some cases, the services may require substantial resources and will affect other incoming services and users; therefore, it is important to make a proper decision for service selection and resources allocation. In service-oriented IoT, an application submitted by a user always requires multiple services or composition of multiple services to fulfil the established goal. Service requests arrive randomly in the system, which causes the uncertainty of services, and the inherent stochastic and dynamic nature of services should be considered in the decision-making process. Therefore, at this layer the authors model the QoS optimization problem as a Markov decision process (MDP). The goal of this process is to maximize the services' quality. Examples of metrics involved in this layer to measure QoS are service cost (the cost to invoke the service), reliability and reputation.

- *Network layer*: At this layer, the QoS module allocates the network resources to the selected services. The authors assume that the network traffic can be classified in two classes: (i) delay or jitter sensitive, denoting services with more strict time requirements, such as real-time-based services, and (ii) BE services, that include all non-detrimental services, such as peer-to-peer applications [48]. Sensitive services require the network layer to provide connections with a minimum transmission rate, while BE services should achieve optimal proportional fairness. The decision-making process at this layer is similar to that of traditional QoS mechanisms in existing networks (such as cellular networks, WSN, and so on), and should consider parameters including human factors (such as stability of service, users, etc.) and technical factors (such as reliability and scalability). An algorithm is used to minimize the connection cost and optimal network attributes, such as bandwidth allocation, network delay and power consumption.
- *Sensing layer*: Per the authors, the characteristics of the sensing layer include (i) autonomy, since the edge-nodes are densely and randomly deployed over the monitored region in an autonomous manner, (ii) limited resources, (iii) susceptibility to the place where the devices are deployed, since in outdoors, remote and hostile areas the devices can be easily damaged, and (iv) the data-centric feature of IoT applications. At this layer, the QoS module is responsible for the selection of basic sensing devices to perform the tasks. In particular, when multiple devices are available that can meet a service request, the decision-making process needs to determine the fittest sensing devices. Such a process is expected to reduce the overlapping of sensing and data redundancy and decrease the energy consumption of devices. The authors consider, among others, the following factors in the decision process: (i) the information accuracy and the sensing coverage required by the application/user should be respected; (ii) links with high bandwidth and low cost have priority for a service; (iii) the number of connections for services should be minimized and the communication load over current communications should be optimized.

Basically, the resource allocation process is tackled as follows: when a service arrives, it is divided into multiple subtasks at the application layer, so that it can be executed over the network layer and then further sent to the sensing layer. In the network layer, a scheduler decides the network type and sensing layer devices, i.e. for data acquisition-based subtasks, the scheduler will arrange the proper RFID or sensor network to execut- them. To support the decision-making process, it is necessary to automatically monitor the QoS attributes. This is done by QoS monitoring modules in the proposed architecture, which are also the core components of their QoS-centric resource management approach. The main functionalities of QoS monitoring modules include the decomposition of the QoS requirements of arriving applications into requirements for individual services, the synthesis of descriptions of QoS attributes among the three layers; and the compilation of the synthesized descriptions into executable subtasks. The final goal of the QoS-centric decision support process is providing flexible and cost-effective services to users/providers.

Another work that emphasises the QoS aspect in the resources managing process for IoT applications is described in [48]. This work focuses on systems composed of heterogeneous infrastructure nodes (in terms of hardware and operating system) that dynamically allocate component-based applications which are also heterogeneous (in terms of implementation language, communication protocols, and QoS requirements). Several key challenges are addressed in the proposal, namely, (i) the adoption of a component framework, (ii) the support for dynamic reconfiguration of components and (iii) the management of the system resources to provide the applications with their required QoS level. The authors propose a middleware solution that addresses these challenges. The proposed middleware inherits the advantages of a standard-based component model and extends it to provide the required QoS-aware reconfiguration support. The QoS characterization is inspired in [49] and extended to model additional aspects such as the application state. More specifically, the middleware extends the distributed applications management plat-form (DAMP) platform introduced in [50]. DAMP provides support for basic life-cycle management of distributed component-based applications, and for node level QoS enforcement in the presence of self-reconfiguration. Based on the support provided by DAMP, the authors propose a holistic approach to the entire system of QoS enforcement through specific resource management policies. They consider the application as a single entity that shares the available resources with the other applications executing on the system. The proposed strategy for QoS management considers the functional dependency between application components, along with their QoS requirements and actual node allocation. Moreover, the eventual avail-ability of redundant component replicas in alternative hardware nodes is considered.

The main mechanism supporting the strategy described in [51] is the self-reconfiguration of components based on external and internal events. Such mechanism relies on four functionalities provided by the extended DAMP platform: (i) monitoring of infrastructure resources, (ii) monitoring of application states, (iii) a reconfiguration API and (iv) a QoS-aware reconfiguration algorithm, this latter being the main contribution of the work. The infrastructure resource monitoring updates the system database with actual node utilization and liveliness information, thus enabling the detection of eventual node overload and physical faults. The application state monitoring collects actual component execution and response times. The system reconfiguration API provides the application components with a mechanism to trigger functional events such as self-QoS change requests and allows the system operator to issue commands for starting and stopping application. The QoS-aware reconfiguration algorithm allocates the available infrastructure resources to the requesting applications, considering their QoS requirements.

The authors consider that a logical component is a functional component that can be deployed in one or more physical nodes. Once deployed, it becomes an actual physical component, and acquires an extra QoS parameter associated with the specific node in which it is deployed. Such parameter is the execution time WCET (worst case execution time of component j in node i, as defined in [49]. When a logical component is deployed in multiple nodes, it is said to be a replicated component. Such redundancy is useful for fault tolerance or load balance purposes. The middleware controls the execution of the components, injects the component state and tunes its QoS parameters. Each component behaves according to a state machine. By using the registry service, a component is registered in the system database and deployed in a specific infrastructure node. Then, it can be launched (instantiated and loaded in memory) by the middleware daemon in response to a command issued through the execution control service exposed by the middleware manager. Once loaded, it can be initialized with specific state and set of QoS parameters. Finally, from this state, the component can be started.

The system registry database stores the QoS model of the system. It considers a set of nodes N that allocate a set of distributed applications A. The cardinality of sets N and A is denoted by $|N|$ and $|A|$, respectively. An application ak is composed of a set of logical components belonging to LC, which is the set of all logical components in the system. Each logical component has its own QoS parameters. The parameters considered in the proposal are period T, deadline D, and priority P. P denotes the QoS priority (criticality), as defined by the system operator at the system configuration stage, and affects the tests for local feasibility performed by the reconfiguration algorithm. The proposed approach is preemptive in the sense that if an application with higher priority enters the system, applications of lower priority will have their QoS degraded or their execution interrupted. $\mathbf{T}$ and $\mathbf{D}$ are vectors with a set of discrete values, representing the period and the deadline of a component. Each possible value pair of $T_{k,j}^{x}$, $D_{k,j}^{x}$ represents a different QoS demand for the component lc$k$. Considering such models, the authors tackle the problem of QoS-aware resource management.

The problem formulation presented in a previous work [50] was extended to include the end-to-end latency of applications and the QoS interdependencies between all applications executing in the system. By taking into account functional and non-functional reconfiguration events, the middleware follows a predefined QoS management policy to allocate the available resources to applications. Such a policy is implemented in a composition algorithm, which can be tuned to meet different needs, for example, optimize the energy consumption, or maximize the system performance. The feasibility of each configuration is verified through a local schedulability test based on the response time analysis (RTA) [52]. The feasibility test is executed in the context of a specific node and considers all the components that are currently executing in the node along with components marked as 'requested for launch' by the composition algorithm. The test returns the estimated node utilization factor if the node configuration is feasible, or a 'nonschedulable' error code if it is not.

In the recently discussed proposal, the authors recognize the importance of considering different priorities (or criticality) of applications while managing resources to be allocated in the IoT system. In their case, the approach assumes that a new application arriving at the system can degrade the performance of applications running that have less priority. This aspect is also investigated in the work described in [53], which consider the application criticality as a major aspect to build IoT systems. The authors in [53] propose an architecture for resource management where sensing and actuation capabilities of devices are shared between applications with different levels of criticality. In the proposal, application criticality defines how essential the application is for the IoT ecosystem. It can be defined either at the application design time by the developer or at runtime by the system administrator. The architecture aims to provide the best possible use of the shared resources while respecting the defined criticalities (priorities of applications).

The proposed resource management architecture can be divided into two levels: System Level and Local Level. All the necessary information about applications and resources are represented with machine-interpretable semantic descriptions based on the semantic web technologies. At the system level, these descriptions are used by the global resource manager for allocating resources to the applications based on their criticality and needs, so that applications defined with the highest level of criticality have priority in the use of resources in detriment to less critical applications. At the local level, each device is assigned with a local resource manager that schedules the access to resources provided by the device so that the performance of the more critical applications could be optimized at the expense of the less critical ones. Figure 5.1 illustrates the proposed architecture.

Applications are software processes that provide different kinds of services for the end users (e.g. turning on the lights in a room when the user enters the room).
Resources are divided into two categories based on their role in the system:

- Sensors: peripheral devices that monitor the status of the environment and provide an interface for accessing such information.
- Actuators: peripheral devices that provide an interface for the applications to modify certain aspects of the physical world.

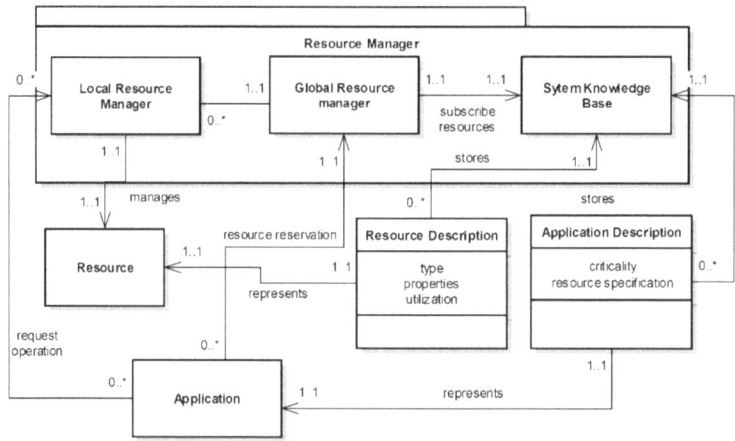

Fig. 5.1 UML diagram representing the system model for resource management in IoT domain as proposed in [53]

Resource and application descriptions represent the information about resources and applications that is relevant for the resource management. **Application descriptions** consist of two main parameters: criticality of the applications and resource specifications. **Resource specifications** describe what kinds of resources are required by the application.

The **resource manager** is a distributed entity consisting of a **system knowledge base (SKB),** a **global resource manager (GRM)** and n number of **local resource manager (LRM)** components (where n is the number of resources in the IoT system), and each resource is equipped with an LRM. The SKB stores the state of the IoT system and provides other components with means to monitor and update such state. The IoT system state represents the applications and resources deployed into the system, as well as the information about which resources are used by the applications in a given time. The GRM manages resources at the system level and aims at optimizing the functionality of the whole IoT system. At local level, the resource management is performed by the LRM, which has the role of authorizing the access to the resource and scheduling the request made by the applications.

The authors do not mention in the paper how the actual resource allocation/ scheduling is realized. They only propose that applications should be described so that their criticality and the required resources are specified, and that the applications most critical are served first. But the authors do not detail any specific algorithm or technique used for the allocation itself. To evaluate the proposed approach in practice, the authors have implemented a reference implementation of the proposed architecture and demonstrated its use through a case study in the context of a smart home environment. The scenario of the case study is composed of three smart lamps, a gateway that communicates with the lamps using ZigBee and that provides a HTTP/JSON based interface for external applications. The demonstration also contains two kinds of applications that utilize the lighting system resource: automatic controller and web user interface (UI). The automatic controller application controls the room lighting automatically, based on the presence of people and time of the day. It has the lowest criticality (200) of the two applications. The UI application is used by two types of users: normal users and admin users. Normal users are assigned with application criticality value of 300. Admin user has the highest criticality (301). The case study showed the use of the architecture when the resources (lamps and gateway) are requested by two different applications (automatic controller and Web user interface) with different levels of criticality. According with the authors, the case study indicates that the proposed approach is suitable for resource management in the IoT domain.

In [54] the authors claim that a novel paradigm built upon context-aware, data- and patient-centric service provision is crucial to deliver personalized healthcare solutions to the elderly and physically challenged. However, this new paradigm requires real-time in-the-field processing of wirelessly collected vital signs using inherently complex physiological models and analysis of the processed information (derived physiological parameters) under a current context (e.g. location, ambient conditions, current physical activity) to extract knowledge about the health condition of patients. As the computational capabilities of biomedical sensor nodes are insufficient to run these complex models, an innovative resource provisioning framework that harnesses the computing capabilities of underutilized electronic devices in the vicinity (e.g. smartphones, laptops, tablets, DVRs, medical terminals) to form a mobile computing grid is proposed in this paper. The framework presents self-optimization and self-healing capabilities for achieving efficiency and robustness even under uncertain conditions. The energy-aware resource provisioning engine endows the self-optimization features while the uncertainty handling mechanism provides the self-healing. A relevant feature of the proposed framework is that it can be used by applications with data parallelism (data is distributed across different parallel computing nodes that perform the same task) as well as by applications with task parallelism (parallel computing nodes may perform different tasks on different data).

The entities that encompass the architecture of the proposed framework can play the following logical roles:

- **Service requester**: responsible for placing requests for workloads that require additional data and/or computing resources from other devices;
- **Service provider**: it can be a data provider, resource provider, or both; data providers provide vital sign and contextual data while resource providers lend their computational (CPU cycles), storage (volatile and non-volatile memory) and communication (i.e. network interface capacity) resources for processing data;

Broker: processes the requests from the requesters, determines the set of service providers that will provide or process data, and distributes the workload of tasks among them. This role can be played by service providers. The broker performs its functions with the aid of a novel energy-aware resource allocation engine, which is responsible to distribute the workload tasks optimally among the service providers. The authors claim the use of multiple brokers, each servicing a different subset of data providers simultaneously, to avoid a single point of failure and to provide redundancy in case some brokers fail. The proper number of brokers is decided by adopting a distributed self-election mechanism.

The brokers are core elements in the proposed framework and are composed of two components: *workload manager* and *scheduler/optimizer*. The first component tracks workload requests, allocates workload tasks among service providers, and aggregates results. The optimizer identifies the number of service providers available for the requested duration and determines the optimal distribution of tasks among them. Different policies can be adopted by the optimizer in its decisions for distributing the workload. A given policy can aim at minimizing the battery drain. Another policy may prioritize the response time without considering battery drain.

Service providers voluntarily advertise their services at the brokers. Service advertisements include information about the current position, amount of computing (in terms of normalized CPU cycles), memory (in Bytes), and communication (in bps) resources, the start and end times of the availability of those resources, and the available battery capacity at each service provider. The brokers know the power drawn by the workload tasks of a specific application when running on a specific class of CPU and memory as well as network resources at each service provider as the information about the different types of devices is known in advance.

When a service requester needs additional data or computing resources, it submits a service request to the nearest broker and also specifies the maximum duration δ max for which it is ready to wait for a service response. The resource allocation engine at the broker determines the associativity of data provider i with service provider j, the list of available resource providers, the duration for which the services of each service provider will be used for data collection, and the duration for which the resources of each service provider will be used for computation and/or multi-hop communication (as a relay node). The objective of the optimization problem is to maximize the minimum residual battery capacity at all the service providers while ensuring that the service response is delivered within δ max. The set of service providers and the duration for which each of their capabilities is available are determined by considering the trade-offs among the cost (in terms of battery drain) for transferring the data locally from data providers to the resource providers, the computational cost for availing the computational capabilities of the resource providers for servicing the request and for aggregating and generating the final response. The framework should ensure that (i) only a resource provider is chosen to perform the computing; (ii) the consumer's deadline for service response is met; (iii) a service provider is utilized only for the duration for which its services are advertised to be available; and (iv) the advertised battery capacity of devices will not be exceeded.

Another important and innovative contribution of [54] regards dealing with uncertainty, very frequent in the IoT context in general, that may affect the resource allocation process. The authors identified two main sources of uncertainties in the application domain investigated and endowed the allocation engine with self-healing properties to guarantee the QoS application (in terms of response time) even in the presence of such uncertainties and the dynamic execution context. The first identified source of uncertainty regards the *inaccuracy in the estimation of task completion times*. Per the authors, this is particularly true when the workload task is submitted by the data provider along with the data and whose behaviour is not known in advance at the broker. In biomedical applications, such type of uncertainty can be minimized by previously profiling the behaviour of the workloads (physiological models). However, some models exhibit radically different behaviours depending on different types of inputs (e.g. sorted/unsorted, dense/sparse) [54]. The second addressed source of uncertainty regards the i*naccurate estimation of the availability (duration) of service providers*. This is typical of any dynamic system such as IoT. The effect of the identified sources of uncertainties is the *over* or *under provision* of resources, both undesired since the former produces waste of resources and the later results in degradation of QoS, or even violation of agreed SLAs. To tackle this issue, the authors introduce the novel idea of *application waypoints*, at which the service providers report to the broker with an estimation of their *residual task completion time.* Such waypoints work as performance or progress indicators. While reporting to the broker, the service providers also specify the next waypoint, i.e. the time at which the broker can expect to hear again from them. If the broker does not receive any feedback from the service provider at these specified waypoints, it marks these service providers as failed after a timeout and assigns additional resources to take over the incomplete tasks.

The paper [55] proposes a resource allocation method using genetic algorithm, which enables the approximation of an optimal solution to the resource allocation problem in IoT. In the proposed architecture, the authors assume that an IoT resource is not able to interact with other resources directly to perform a given task. Instead, all interactions between resources can be done only via service gateways, which are deployed in an IoT environment along with the IoT resources. Therefore, as in the initial view of IoT, in this proposal the authors consider as IoT resources only the very constrained things that are not able to provide computational services. A service gateway is a computation node that runs service instances. It relays communication between IoT resources to execute a user requested task. If there is an IoT device endowed with the networking and computational capabilities to be part of a mobile and ad hoc network and to run service instances, they regard it as a service gateway as well.

The proposed system model encompasses IoT resources, service gateways, and the connections between them. These components are deployed in an environment to perform a user requested task, which is defined as a composite service. A composite service consists of service instances which are instantiated by making bindings to IoT resources that are necessary to provide their capabilities [55]. The execution of a composite service depends on the interactions and data exchange between IoT resources. The amount of data that needs to be transmitted between services is determined in runtime based on their execution history, and it can change during the execution. Each IoT resource must be allocated to at least (or possible more than) one gateway to transmit data to other IoT resources in order to execute a composite service. The number of IoT resources that can be allocated to a given gateway is constrained by the gateway *resource connection capacity*. IoT resources that are allocated to different gateways can communicate with each other via gateway connections. All the gateways in the IoT system can communicate among themselves either direct or indirectly. The number of direct connections with other gateways is limited by the *gateway connection capacity*.

From the foregoing description, it is clear that in [55], the IoT devices are separated into two distinct types. One type consists of devices with extremely limited resources and incapable of providing data processing functions. Such devices are considered as providers of sensing resource only (data sources), which serve as input for the processing functions. The other type of devices, called service gateways, are more computationally powerful and actively participate in the provision of resources for the effective execution of the user requested tasks. In addition, they manage all the exchange of resources among the most restricted devices, as required for the task execution. Several works also assume the existence of two categories of IoT devices. Moreover, the presence of a resource rich gateway, also called Smart Gateway or IoT Gateway [56] is considered in various proposals. According to the authors in [57], except for the most basic sensors, IoT devices are typically equipped with storage capacities and execution environments that, although limited, are able to carry out important parts of the application tasks. Taking into account the capabilities of these devices relatively rich in resources is essential to enable large-scale IoT systems, such as in the smart city domain. Thus, by exploiting the capabilities of IoT service gateways, in [55] the application tasks are entirely performed by the interconnected things without resorting to external systems such as clouds. However, the distinction between the two types of devices features the heterogeneity of the system. In this context, the problem addressed by the authors consists in determining the resource allocation scheme and finding the gateway connections that minimize data transmission between gateways during the execution of a composite service. They modelled the resource allocation problem as a variant of the degree constrained minimum-spanning tree problem and applied a genetic algorithm to reduce the time required to produce a near-optimal solution. They defined a fitness function and an encoding scheme for the candidate solutions to apply the genetic algorithm in an efficient way.

The authors in [58] present their proposal for task mapping specifically tailored for IoT scenarios. The authors share our view that, although IoT inherits several characteristics from WSNs, it also introduces its own particular features, and they formalize the task mapping problem addressing IoT specific needs. First, they consider the IoT requirements of sharing Things (and their related sensing data) between multiple users, thus bringing out the need to manage the concurrence between tasks. Second, as users make their devices available for shared processing, new constraints emerge, for instance to control the amount of resources allocated to the tasks of other users and to distributed tasks among the network in a fair way in order to avoid exhausting some specific nodes (load balancing). The authors emphasize the heterogeneity of IoT devices and applications, and the consequent variety of operations required to be performed by the system, demanding different amounts of resources and times to be completed. Finally, they pay special attention to the fact that IoT devices produce endless data streams that require continuous processing, respecting the accuracy and time constrains dictated by applications while minimizing the energy consumption. Considering all the above-mentioned features, the authors formulate a new task mapping problem according to the specifics of the IoT, by generalizing the existing system models (i.e., the way to describe tasks and devices) for WSNs and cloud computing under a comprehensive and unified IoT system model [58]. Their proposed approach simultaneously handles constraints associated with embedded systems (minimize energy consumption and wireless network communication in a resource-constrained environment), shared sensing (concurrent tasks and load balancing) and continuous processing (varying resource consumption, unbounded data streams) in a heterogeneous and large-scale mobile network (various hardware and software functionalities available, location-aware devices and QoS constraints).

Globally, the task mapping problem consists in finding the best way to allocate a *task* on a set of *nodes* (the Things). As the IoT is an extension of the Internet, and can involve any device able to perform sensing or processing tasks (including, e.g. computer grids and the cloud), the set of nodes is a subset of eligible nodes with respect to the task. The authors assume that this subset is given by an external registry, which references the nodes and can be requested to get those that match specific properties. One remarkable feature of this work is that it is one of the few reported in the surveyed literature to specifically consider actuation tasks in their model. Actuation operations are essential in the IoT vision but still neglected in most resource allocation proposals. In [58], an IoT-centric task is a composition of *operations* subdivided into sensing, processing and actuation. Two operations a and b can be linked together by a *stream*, which establishes a precedence relationship between them: a datum produced by a causes a reaction from b. The mapping must then consider all the characteristics and *constraints* expressed by each operation, so that they are assigned to nodes that meet the required properties (type and amount of resources, location, etc.). In addition, as Things are shared, many operations can coexist on a Thing when a new one is deployed. Consequently, every mapping computation depends on previous ones, i.e. a mapping computed at time t must take account of all the tasks that have been deployed on each Thing since the time they were turned on.

Another differential of their proposal is the explicit representation of data streams. The authors define a *stream s* as an infinite sequence indexed by t (timestamps), and where each term (It) is a *stream item*, i.e. a measurement sensed from the real world. They denote the set of all streams as s, and the set of all items producible by a stream s as Is. Similarly, they use $s(x)$ to denote the finite sub-sequence of (It) where $t0 \leq t \leq x$ (i.e. the set of items produced by a stream s between the time $t0$ and the time x), and $|s(x)|$ its size. In this new sequence, the order of the terms is preserved by the time relationship that exists in $s = $ (It). The number of items produced by a stream can vary over time, and its average throughput is denoted as $\rho = \lim t \to \infty |s(t)| \div t$. The function $\rho(t)$ describes the throughput variations, by associating at each time t, the corresponding number of items produced per second.

In the same way as in several other studies, in [58] a *task* is modelled as a directed acyclic graph (DAG) encompassing a set of operations. The edges linking such operations represent a data stream that flows from one operation (the stream producer) to the subsequent one (the stream consumer). Their model includes the description of the resources required by each operation along time. Then, unlike most approaches that split the continuous data processing into discrete cycles, the authors believe that continuous consumption of resources should be modelled as continuous functions rather than constants to increase the accuracy of the mapping. They claim that the effective throughput of the operations over data streams can vary quickly, constantly affecting the need for memory or computation power. Therefore, they adopt two functions (shaped as constant or increasing functions) to express the requirements in terms of memory and disc space (in bytes) of each operation between the deployment of the task graph and a given time t. Another function models the number of instructions per second (ips) required to compute the operation at each time t. Two other functions model the energy consumption with computation and with communication, both considering the real throughput of the output streams. In addition, the model allows expressing a set of *constraints* to specify the operation requirements regarding the execution environment, for instance, geographic location, specific type of hardware, software or sensing devices, sample rate, accuracy, response time and other QoS constraints as communication reliability, computation time and security. They represent all these constrains in a simple way, as a binary function, in which a given node n either satisfies (value = 1) or does not satisfy (value = 0) such a function.

The authors model the set of nodes encompassing the IoT system along with the current status of their resource consumptions, which depends on the operations being executed on each node. The functions used to model the resource consumptions allows anticipating the future state, and can be approximated as the sum of consumed resources by each operation deployed on the node. Therefore, the task mapping problem consists in finding a mapping that maximizes/minimizes some target properties, while satisfying all the constraints of the operations, without exceeding the available amount of resources. Again, they differentiate their proposal from traditional WSN task mapping, in which the main goal of any decision is to minimize the overall energy consumption. Their proposal instead favours the fair distribution of operations inside the network, by reducing the probability that an operation is mapped on a node when this node is already loaded. Therefore, they formulate the task mapping problem in the IoT as consisting in (i) minimizing the consumption of resources by each Thing in the network and (ii) load balancing the operations among the nodes. For this purpose, they introduce four objective functions that must be minimized. These functions evaluate the consumption of each resource (energy, memory, cpu and disk). To reduce the complexity of multi-objective programming, an aggregation function G is used to combine the results of the four objective functions. They use a sum in the paper, but G can be any polynomial function (e.g. weighted sum or quadratic polynomial) provided as a parameter of the task mapping process. Using G, finding a task mapping can be formulated as a binary programming problem [59], since the decision variables are only binary. Binary linear programming problems can be solved optimally; this can however, be highly time-consuming in practice. As a solution, the authors introduce a heuristic and a greedy algorithm that (i) solve the problem in a reasonably short time and (ii) is simple enough to be executed opportunistically in the network by a set of fairly powerful *things* elected dynamically.

In [60] the authors assume that an IoT device consists of multiple network interfaces of heterogeneous technologies. Each interface provides a set of non-interchangeable resources which are demanded by a given set of services. Services are flexible in the sense that they can be split between more than one interface. The authors model the assignment of services to the interfaces and call this problem as the *Service-to-Interface Assignment* (SIA). In the paper, they characterize the complexity for solving this problem and also provide fast algorithms which are compared with the optimal solution. The authors present a MILP formulation of the SIA problem considering heterogeneous resources. The goal of solving the problem is to minimize the total cost of utilizing the interfaces' resources, while satisfying the services' requirements. They consider the total cost as the sum of the cost of utilizing each resource unit along with the activation of each interface being engaged to serve a service. In their system model, the authors represent the resources associated with each interface of a device (for example CPU cycles, downlink data rate, buffer size). They use a simple attribute-based for their resource model. They assume that each service is associated with a K-dimensioned demand integer vector and, likewise, each interface has a K-dimensioned capacity (resource availability) integer vector. To model the burden imposed on the operating system of the device to handle the services split through its interfaces, they introduce a fixed-cost factor called the activation cost per interface. This is employed as a parameter to gauge the number of splits. Aside from this fixed cost, they also consider a utilization cost per unit of resource used on an interface. Moreover, they assume that each service j incurs an overhead on the resource it utilizes, which may vary by interface to capture MAC and PHY layer practical considerations. Their final goal is to serve all demands by assigning them to the physical interfaces, minimizing the total cost of using them, namely the total resource utilization and activation cost. In the paper, they prove the NP-completeness of the problem. For reasonable instance sizes, the presented formulation produces optimal solutions. They address two cases; (i) when the interfaces have enough available resources to serve the demands in one round, and (ii) when the interfaces need to serve the demands in multiple rounds, i.e. serving a partial amount of the demands in each round. They develop two algorithms to approximate the optimal solution for large instance sizes. The first algorithm allocates the most demanding service requirements first, taking into consideration the average cost of utilizing interface resources, while the second one calculates the demanding resource shares and allocates the most demanding of them first by choosing randomly among equally demanding shares.

In [61] the authors claim that the ultimate goal of an IoT system is to enable the network objects to dynamically cooperate and make their resources available, in order to reach a goal, i.e. the execution of one or more applications assigned to the network. In this context, they first define the problem of resource allocation for the deployment of distributed applications in heterogeneous networks, and the challenges related to this problem. In particular, they emphasize the challenges of dealing with the large-scale, distributed and heterogeneous nature of IoT networks, as well as the dynamic behaviour of their nodes, that leads to the preponderance of opportunistic networking and opportunistic sensing. They argue that in such a dynamic, large-scale and heterogeneous environment, it is not reasonable that resource allocation is performed in a centralized way. Based on their initial considerations, the authors describe the architecture of their proposed middleware that enables the deployment of IoT applications to network resources, based on a distributed and coordinated negotiation among network objects. The authors propose a distributed protocol based on the consensus algorithm, and adapt it to solve the problem of resource allocation and management in IoT. They focus on adjusting sensing functionalities of IoT nodes so that resources are equally shared among nodes participating into the execution of a given application.

In the proposal, the authors adopt a virtualization-based approach for modelling resources and use the concept of virtual objects (VO). Although the paper does not provide details on how to specify VOs, in short, the physical nodes are grouped by the type of task they can perform and a VO is assigned to control groups of nodes. A VO is responsible for keeping track of the physical nodes that belong to the same task group (i.e. groups of nodes performing similar and mutually replaceable tasks). In the proposed architecture, there is a central server (a.k.a. leader node), responsible for transmitting an activation signal to VOs. Each VO is aware of which nodes the activation signal is addressed to. Therefore, it is able to forward the activation signal to the appropriate nodes, based on the information of the task group the nodes belong to. The aim of the proposed algorithm is, for each node belonging to the same task group, to dynamically assign each task in order to share the effort required to perform it, in terms of necessary resources. The assignment decision is based on the application of the consensus algorithm proposed in [62]. The original algorithm was devised for clock synchronization among nodes in a WSN. It was adapted in [61] to solve the problem of resource allocation and management in IoT systems.

The consensus algorithm consists in a collection of laws that regulates the interaction and the exchange of information between nodes in a group which needs to reach a coordination to achieve common goals. All nodes in the network use the same algorithm in order to make decisions according to information available both locally and received from other nodes [61]. In the consensus-based task allocation proposal described in [61] the authors define a resource utilization model to represent the power consumption with tasks. The model considers the frequency with which each node i collects data during the execution of a task and the energy consumed by the node as a function of the energy consumed per task. It also considers the amount of data collected by node per task at a given time t, as a function of the output data for the task and the buffer occupancy of the node. Then, the models specified for the data sensing process are simplified by considering the first order dynamic of node i. In such simplification, the number of samples collected by node i is given by the sum of the local task slope, which determines the task frequency, multiplied by the time, and the local bias that describes the number of samples stored in the node buffer. The final objective of the formulated problem is to obtain the same virtual dynamic on all nodes. Every node keeps an estimation of the virtual dynamic using a linear function of its own local function. So, the goal is to find values for the local function of the nodes that compensate the difference among all node dynamics. To reach this goal, the adapted consensus algorithm is applied. The consensus algorithm is implemented by the nodes within each task group and entails an iterative procedure that updates the slope and bias values. There are three different approaches for the algorithm application. In the *single task–single frequency* approach, the goal is to make the nodes within the task group to agree on a common frequency for the execution of only the relevant task. In the *single task–total frequency* approach, the goal is to make the nodes agree on the frequency for the execution of all tasks. Finally, in the *entire network* approach, the goal is to achieve an intergroup agreement.

5.4.3   Discussion

As aforementioned, IoT shares several characteristics of WSN. Both are networks encompassing a large number of heterogeneous, resource-constrained and battery-powered devices collecting environmental data through sensors, continuously processing them, and possibly controlling actuators to react on the physical world upon receiving a stimulus. On the one hand, we can consider WSN as a key enabler of IoT, since the sensor nodes provide the core functionality of sensing the environment and the wireless links provide an essential part of the communication infrastructure. On the other hand, it is still possible to have an IoT ecosystem without a WSN, for instance in the case of RFIDs or systems composed of smartphones.

In WSNs, since wireless communication is a major source of energy consumption, in-network processing is usually exploited to increase the network lifetime by locally processing data and avoiding unnecessary data transmission to centralized collection points. In the same way, in an IoT system, the computational resources of the devices should be exploited to perform local processing. In particular, the ever evolving category of smart devices, such as smart TVs and smartphones, offers increasing processing and storage resources [63]. Therefore, decisions on resource allocation and task scheduling must consider the IoT devices as potential nodes to be assigned tasks. Each node participating as an IoT system device should be regarded as an active entity capable of providing one or more of the three types of resources (networking, compute or storage), instead of only acting as passive data provider. This feature makes the decision-making process regarding the selection of the most suitable devices to perform the application tasks a complex problem.

If we consider that WSNs are a part of an IoT ecosystem, undoubtedly existing solutions for resource allocation in WSN are useful and fit into the IoT context. Indeed, as we discussed earlier, there are proposals such as [44] that specifically address the research directions necessary to circumvent the limitations of legacy WSNs and evolve them as truly enabling technologies for IoT. However, we claim that there are some differences between IoT and WSN that require specific approaches in order to achieve an integrated and holistic solution to this emerging field. In Chap. 2, we listed the key requirements of IoT to be considered in the broader context of resource management. Now we will discuss these requirements again, but in the narrower context of resource allocation, and emphasizing the differences comparing to the WSN field. We will also illustrate how the studies discussed above in this section address each requirement.

Scale. Traditional WSNs were often application-specific systems, restricted to a regional scale, and not necessarily connected to the Internet. Although this application-specific design for WSNs is evolving towards shared sensor networks [64] and/or virtualized sensor networks approaches [41], the scale of a sensor network is still typically limited. On the other hand, as the Internet itself was designed to be a network of networks, also IoT is a global, ultra large-scale system, often encompassing (but not restricted to) several WSNs. IoT applications, such as smart roads, smart metering, digital factory, smart city, just to name a few, will require tens of thousands of sensors and actuators. Such scale factor brings new challenges such as, for instance, the need of adopting distributed solutions to the resource allocation/task scheduling problem, since centralized solutions are not feasible in such a scenario. In the discussed proposals, the most widely used approach to address scalability consisted of organizing the system intelligence in a hierarchy, with at least two levels of decision making regarding the resource allocation: one at a global scale and the other at a local scale. The implementation of the resource management system (RMS) on two levels (global and local) is adopted in [46, 53]. In a similar way, the work in [54] adopts multiple Brokers in order to assure both the scale and the redundancy of system resources (thus contributing to fault tolerance).

High degree of heterogeneity. The heterogeneity of devices has always been considered as a major challenge in the WSN field. Such heterogeneity concerns various types of sensor platforms, communication protocols, operating systems and programming environments. In IoT, the heterogeneity of devices gains a new dimension, since it is assumed that virtually any type of object on earth can participate in an IoT ecosystem. So, the need to tackle interoperability issues and to provide abstractions to describe resources and applications are challenging research issues. Specifically, in the context of the resource allocation activity, heterogeneity affects the solutions about managing the collaboration between the various players. Ad hoc networks can be formed by the interaction of nodes from a WSN with mobile phones, domestic appliances, smart vehicles, and the resources need to be exchanged between these objects to respect their individual limitations, while efficiently exploiting their capabilities, and always aiming at the highest goal to meet the application requirements. In fact, not only IoT devices (*things*) actively participate as resources to perform the applications tasks, but all the other layers of the ecosystem, including gateways, edge nodes and data centres of computational clouds, should be considered. The discussed proposals deal with this high degree of heterogeneity mainly by employing virtualization [41, 61] and middleware approaches [46, 51].

Mobility, dynamic context and opportunistic interactions. Although there are application domains where the monitored phenomenon is mobile, and therefore the resource allocation solutions must consider the mobility factor, most proposals for WSN do not address such an issue. Existing solutions deal with the mobility of devices only partially, more like a part of the dynamic execution context of these networks. In general, the approach to deal with the dynamic contextual changes is to assume the task allocation scheme/algorithm runs periodically in several cycles (rounds), and receives as input the updated context information from the network nodes. Among such context information, the current location of devices can be included, thus being part of a solution to handle mobility. In IoT, however, the mobility of devices is an essential part of a resource allocation solution. On the one hand, the presence of devices moving through the environment, often at high speed and following random paths, brings a huge management challenge. On the other hand, it brings new opportunities that can be exploited. An interesting example discussed in [44] takes advantage of idle resources of devices that have greater computational capacity and are located in the vicinity of a given resource con-strained node, to perform tasks that require more complex processing than such node would be able to perform alone. This behaviour characterizes opportunistic interactions that depend on the current device context, including its location. IoT devices could, at given times, associate themselves with resources in their vicinity, thus changing their resource pool over time [44]. These interactions can be further exploited to create clusters or clouds, of devices, which can cooperate in an ad hoc basis, subject to mobility and other contextual changes, to meet the application requirements. Sharing the resources of such an opportunistic pool of devices that move in the space, potentially contributes to increase the resource utilization, but also enables new types of applications [17]. This type of interaction is not usually explored in the WSN field, but as we saw in the aforementioned example, it can bring many benefits in terms of increasing the aggregate capacity of resource provision in an IoT ecosystem. Besides exploiting mobility and opportunistic interactions, other types of context (in addition to location) can also affect the resource allocation strategy. Works such as [46, 51, 54] monitor the execution environment in terms of different parameters (as application requirements, residual energy, etc.) and keep update contextual information in order to improve their decisions on resource allocation. By using information on the current available resources, more cost-effective decisions can be taken. Moreover, the context awareness is a key feature to build truly autonomic IoT systems, able to react to failures in devices or communication links, new requirements, and to exploit optimization opportunities without requiring manual intervention.

Complexity in the management of QoS requirements. QoS requirements traditionally used in computer networks are not sufficient for IoT systems. These general requirements mainly relate to network characteristics, such as bandwidth, delay or jitter, which are only part of the QoS problem to be managed in IoT. Requirements in the IoT domain need to be treated with a multi-level approach. Meeting the application requirements is the ultimate goal of any cyber-physical system, without which the actual construction of the system makes no sense. Therefore, these requirements must guide all decisions on the allocation of system resources. However, application requirements are generally expressed in an abstract way, linked to the application domain and the user high-level goals. To satisfy them, all parts of the system need to collaborate by addressing specific concrete requirements that make sense in their own different contexts. For example, the network will need to provide communication services that meet the traditional network requirements. However, the sensing devices will also need to meet requirements such as accuracy of information and sensing coverage. At the same time, there are general requirements for systems that run on devices with limited resources, such as minimizing the energy consumption to increase their durability, which should also be considered. There should be, therefore, mechanisms to allow the representation of QoS requirements at different levels and to properly map between them. After the established requirements, the various components of a

RAS will need to cooperate to ensure that the services are provided in order to fulfil them. There is still no consensus on the definition of QoS in IoT, this being an open research question that has been exploited by recent works, as we discussed above, where most of the proposals [46, 48, 51, 53, 54, 58] considered QoS requirements as key features in their RMS. Works such as [48] adopt a QoS-centric approach in which the QoS requirements guide the entire allocation process. Among relevant QoS parameters, latency is considered by some works as a primer requirement [51]. Indeed, time critical applications demand more resources from the system and the allocation strategy needs to employ fast algorithms to properly meet them.

Multiple and heterogeneous applications. As aforementioned, the first generations of WSNs were designed by adopting a fit for purpose approach. The owner of the network was in general the owner of the application and the entire building of the system was tied to the requirements of such target application. Reuse of artefacts and resource sharing were not stimulated. With the new generation of WSNs, the focus is increasingly changed to transform the sensor node infrastructure into resource providers, which are shared, often using virtualization, by multiple applications. In such a scenario, the distinction between WSNs and IoT becomes increasingly blurred. However, while the solutions to virtualize WSNs and share their resources among applications are still in the early stages, the IoT has been originally conceived as an ecosystem oriented towards multiple applications. Such applications are inherently heterogeneous in terms of their functional and non-functional requirements, and run concurrently on the network, contending for the available resources. Therefore, a crucial issue concerns managing the simultaneous satisfaction of their requirements and consider the various priorities, or criticality of applications. Certainly, an application that monitors the vital signs of a patient, or a fire detection application, are more critical than an application that only enhances the comfort of the users. Applications with the highest level of criticality need to have their requirements met with highest priority. Therefore, solutions for resource allocation in IoT must provide mechanisms to represent the priorities of the applications and to ensure that these priorities are respected when making the task scheduling. The approaches presented in [51, 53] propose promising solutions to accommodate different priorities of applications.

Data stream-oriented and real-time processing. Although the data generated by sensors are inherently streams, most works from the WSN field do not effectively exploit the particularities of this type of processing in scheduling decisions. The bursty nature, variable throughputs of data streams, the spatiotemporal correlations between data samples, are all factors that affect the task scheduling. There is need for continuous processing, which preferably calls for online solutions. It is also need to deal with partial and inaccurate query results. WSN works in general neglect these aspects. Existing proposals consider that the system execution is divided into cycles or rounds, and the assignment of tasks is made with respect to the current cycle, regardless of the influence of past system states. However, such approach does not consider the specific nature of the data streams, and can generate inefficient results of resource allocation or the failure to meet the application requirements. The proposal presented in [58] was the only one we found in our literature search that fully addresses the requirement of data stream processing. The proposal described in [54] addresses real-time data processing only because this is a strict requirement in the considered application domain (an eHealth application). However, such work does not give emphasis to the data stream characteristic of the sensing data; instead their focus is on meeting the hard real-time constrains posed in the resource allocation process.

Another feature of IoT that may affect resource allocation decisions refers to the fact that its topology is both unknown and dynamic [65]. The devices that make up a IoT ecosystem can enter and leave the system opportunistically, due to various factors such as mobility, battery exhaustion or simply by the user's decision to turn off his/her device. This makes the availability of resources and services provided by such devices highly variable. As a consequence, it can be very hard for a RMS to precisely estimate the time for a task completion, since the nodes responsible for performing such task can be suddenly unavailable. Moreover, this can also produce incompleteness in the produced data. For example, there may be a loss of some data-points during the continuous collection of a data stream as a result of the temporary unavailability of the source devices. Coupled with the sensor data inherent characteristic of being noisy and inaccurate, there is an uncertainty factor in the IoT data that needs to be considered to meet the application requirements. From the studies discussed above, only [54] takes into account this feature and provides mechanisms to deal with the inaccuracy in both the estimation of task completion times and of the availability of service providers during the resource allocation activity.

In addition to all the aspects discussed briefly above, and investigated by some described proposals, another important difference between IoT and WSN systems is the role of gateway nodes. In WSN, the main role of gateways is acting as bridges between the sensor nodes and external systems (as the Internet). They are responsible for receiving the application requests, translating them to commands to be issued to the nodes and then reporting the results (sensing data) back to the application. Scheduling decisions can be performed by the gateway (in centralized solutions) and then the allocation of tasks is communicated to the sensor nodes, which will effectively perform all the necessary sensing and processing tasks. As it is assumed the adoption of *in networking* processing, the gateway basically per-forms communication tasks. In IoT, some studies also adopt the approach in which a gateway is only a bridge between devices and other systems. Or in other words, it is a node responsible for bridging the data acquisition and data processing tasks. These works generally assume that IoT devices have very limited resources and are merely passive data sources, while more computationally powerful systems will perform all data processing. However, in proposals such as [55] the gateway is seen as another type of device pertaining to the Thing tier of an IoT system architecture, one with more powerful resources. As such, the gateway also receives processing load, not only communication tasks. Accordingly, they also need to be considered as resource providers to be managed and taken into account by the RMS.

Table 5.3 summarises the discussed challenges involved in IoT resource allo-cation and the studies adopting an *IoT only* approach that tackled them. Besides the

Table 5.3 Comparison of approaches for IoT only

IoT requirements		Papers										
		[41]	[44]	[46]	[48]	[51]	[53]	[54]	[55]	[58]	[60]	[61]
High scale		✓		✓			✓			✓		
Heterogeneity	Devices	✓	✓	✓	✓	✓	✓	✓	✓	✓	✓	✓
	Applications	✓	✓	✓	✓	✓	✓	✓	✓	✓	✓	✓
Data stream processing										✓		
Real-time processing								✓		✓		
Dynamic environment			✓	✓	✓	✓	✓	✓	✓	✓	✓	✓
Opportunistic interactions			✓					✓		✓		
Complex QoS requirements				✓	✓	✓	✓	✓		✓		
Context/location-awareness			✓	✓		✓	✓	✓		✓		
Mobility			✓					✓	✓	✓		
Fault tolerance						✓		✓	✓			
Application priority						✓	✓					
Load balance			✓			✓				✓		

features listed as key requirements for resource management in IoT, the table encompasses additional features addressed by the proposals for resource allocation described in Sect. 5.4. We can observe that the most comprehensive proposal is [58], which tackles almost all the issues we have discussed here. Moreover, we can notice that heterogeneity is a key issue, tackled by all studies analysed in this section. QoS management is also addressed by almost all proposals. A surprising observation regards the scalability issue. Although recognized as a key feature of IoT systems, few proposals discussed in this section explicitly mention solutions tailored to deal with such issue. The high distribution of devices in IoT and the inherent decentralized processing naturally contribute to promote the scalability of the system to a certain extent. However, to achieve the true ultra-scale envisioned for IoT, we believe that solutions categorized as IoT only have a serious drawback. Even considering the presence of resource rich IoT devices (gateways), the workload generated by the huge number of interconnected devices will probably overload the system. Real-time requirements, complex data analytics and processing involving geographically dispersed data are unlikely to be met without resorting to more powerful devices as the cloud macro data centres or edge micro data centres.

5.5 Managing Resources at the Edge: The Need for an Intermediate Tier

In this section, we discuss proposals for resource allocation in IoT that assume the presence of an intermediate tier, resulting from the increasing need of managing resources at the edge of the network, in the halfway from the data sources and remote cloud data centres. Traditional gateways evolved to smart gateways which finally were interconnected and augmented with new responsibilities to compose a whole new intermediate layer of networking and processing. The approach to bringing computational resources to the edge of the networks, thus closer to the end user, has been extensively investigated in recent literature under different monikers, such as Edge computing [66], mobile edge computing [67], fog computing [68], cloudlets [69] and containerization [70]. In such proposals, edge/fog nodes are important players in the resource allocation process, acting both as decision makers for the task assignments and as active service providers.

Edge computing is not necessarily applied only in IoT scenarios, but as several authors have pointed out, its usage perfectly accommodates several requirements of IoT in terms of the resource management. According to the authors in [71], fog computing fits perfectly with the IoT paradigm, mainly for the following reasons: (i) the privileged position of the fog/edge nodes, between the Things and the cloud tiers, thus providing better performance in terms of delay; (ii) the distributed nature of the micro data centres, in contrast to the centralized nature of the more expensive cloud data centres, which promotes better scalability and resilience for the fog, (iii) the support to mobility, (iv) the potential to provide real-time data processing and (v) on the fly data analysis, for instance by performing data aggregation to send partially processed data as opposed to send raw data to the cloud data centres for further processing. Moreover, by adopting an intermediate fog tier in a three-tier system architecture, it is possible to avoid the cloud lock-in problem [72], since Fog resources can interoperate with various cloud providers.

5.5.1 Examples of Edge-Based Approaches

The authors in [73] adopt a system architectural for IoT systems in which they consider the presence of a Smart Gateway along with a fog layer. In their approach, the fog layer refers to a set of distributed resources located in a so-called smart network. In their paper, they first motivate for the need of more than a single Gateway in IoT scenarios, as we have already discussed above. Considering the high complexity of tasks that a Smart Gateway must perform, the authors claim that fog computing can play an important role to alleviate this burden from gateways. Mainly in the large-scale, multi-hop communication IoT systems, probably it will not be feasible for a single gateway perform all required tasks. Therefore, temporary storage, pre-processing, data security and privacy related tasks, and others can be done more easily and efficiently in the presence of a smart network or fog, co-located with the Smart Gateway. They claim that the fog layer provides low latency communication and context awareness capabilities. Moreover, it allows real-time delivery of data, especially for delay sensitive and healthcare-related applications. In this context, the authors propose a layered architecture for Smart Gateways, encompassing six logical layers. Their focus was on presenting the underpinning architectural blocks to enable their view and on assessing the communication between the gateway and the cloud. In the **physical and virtualization layer**, physical nodes, WSNs, virtual nodes, and virtual sensor networks are managed and maintained according to the needs of applications. The **monitoring layer** monitors the activities of the underlying nodes and networks, by keeping track of which node is performing what task, at what time and also of the energy consumption to perform such tasks. This layer is probably responsible for the resource allocation functions in the proposed architecture. However, the authors do not mention in the paper any specific approach, algorithm or strategy being used to make the decisions about which device will perform which task and when. The **pre-processing layer** performs tasks related to data management. It analyses the collected data, performs data filtering, trimming and other functions to generate more meaningful and useful data to be consumed by applications/users. Data is then temporarily stored on the fog resources (**Temporary Storage Layer**). Once the data is uploaded on the cloud and it is no more required to be locally stored, it is then removed from the storage media. The **security layer** addresses issues regarding data privacy and location-awareness, but this is not detailed in the paper. Finally, the **transport layer** is in charge of uploading the ready-to-send data to the cloud, burdening the core to the minimum and delivering more useful services to end users.

Another work that leverages the concept of making computational resources available at the edge of the network is described in [74], with focus on data stream processing. According to the authors [74], with the emergence of fog computing, the widespread resources located in smaller data centres at the edges of the network are changing the landscape of traditional data stream processing (DSP) platforms. They envision a distributed DSP system spread among multiple small data centres sparse in the urban environment, and located close to the data sources but with non-negligible network latency among them. The authors claim that to fully exploit the potential of such infrastructure, a distributed DSP system should be enhanced with a scheduler that is tailored to the novel requirements posed by this scenario. This scheduler needs to assign the stream processing elements in a network-aware and scalable fashion, while considering several QoS attributes. In this context, they propose a distributed and self-adaptive QoS-aware scheduler for Storm [75], an open source, real-time, distributed and resilient DSP system. Their proposal is specifically tailored for scenarios when Storm is deployed on an infrastructure with non-negligible latencies, such as envisioned for a Fog integrated IoT system.

In the proposal, the scheduler is a core component of a DSP system, responsible for the decision-making process regarding the task assignments. A DSP application is represented by a directed acyclic graph (DAG), where the vertices are the application operators, and the edges are the data streams exchanged between operators. For execution, a DSP is instantiated in a distributed infrastructure, which consists of a set of worker nodes, i.e. computational resources, interconnected by an overlay network [74]. The scheduler is then in charge of solving the operator placement problem consisting in determining the nodes that should host and execute the DSP operators. To solve the posed problem, the authors implemented a QoS-aware distributed scheduling algorithm by adapting to Storm the network-aware scheduling algorithm proposed by Pietzuch et al. [76]. The algorithm comprises a cost space, which models the placement problem by transforming the performance metrics of interest into distances over this space, and an operator placement algorithm, which places operators in this cost space. The metrics considered in the problem formulation are the network usage, utilization and availability. The former captures the node processing latency, which is a function of the node utilization level. The latter represents the fraction of time a node is up and able to execute the required operations. The operator placement comprises an initial phase of virtual operator placement, where operators are placed in the cost space, and a subsequent phase of physical operator mapping, where the decision is reflected back to a physical node. As a modification of the original algorithm, since different applications can be differently affected by the performance attributes considered (latency, availability and utilization), the authors introduced a set of weights. These weights allow tuning the relative importance of the different attributes for each specific application.

Besides proposing the modified algorithm, the authors extended the Storm architecture by including new modules. In particular, the proposed scheduler with QoS-awareness and adaptability features was implemented as a component called **AdaptiveScheduler**. The **AdaptiveScheduler** is located on each worker node and executes the distributed scheduling policy. Another component included in the Storm architecture to implement the operator placement strategy is the **QoSMonitor**. This component is responsible for gathering all the information necessary for the QoS-aware decision process. It estimates the network latency with the other system nodes and monitors the QoS attributes of the worker node, i.e. node availability utilization. They also introduced a **WorkerMonitor** for each Storm worker process, which computes and stores incoming and outgoing data rates; this information is used by the scheduler to compute the value of data rate over a link. In the **AdaptiveScheduler**, the original algorithm proposed in [76] was adjusted to account for the specific Storm application model. This component was designed as a classical adaptive software system, which reacts to internal and external changes of the operating conditions through a feedback control loop based on the MAPE reference model for autonomic systems [77]. The monitor phase of the MAPE control loop starts with the analysis of the information collected by the QoSMonitor in order to identify the set of local executors that can be moved, i.e. are not pinned, not assigned to be moved by other Storm scheduling entity, and not directly connected to an operator which is going to be reassigned. Next, for each local executor in the list of movable candidates, the AdaptiveScheduler runs the virtual placement algorithm, starting the analyse phase. The goal of this phase is to determine whether the local executors identified as movable candidate will be effectively moved to another position. For those executors that are to be moved to a new position, the algorithm triggers the plan phase. The goal of the plan phase is to determine which worker node will execute the local executor e_i. To this end, the physical placement algorithm tries to locate the worker node closest to the position of t e_i which has at least a free worker slot and can thus host e_i. If no worker node is found, the MAPE iteration for executor e_i finishes. Finally, the execute phase is in charge of moving e_i to the new candidate node. The new assignment decision is shared with the involved worker nodes. The adoption of the MAPE-based feedback loop for adaptation and of the multi-dimensional cost space allows the **AdaptiveScheduler** to manage changes occurring both in the infrastructure layer (e.g. new worker nodes that appear or existing ones that fail) and in the application layer (e.g. increase in the source data rate).

Another work that adopts an intermediate layer at the network edge for processing the application workload in IoT is described in [78], although the focus of their proposal is only on the communication resources of the system. Such work was proposed in the context of an important application domain, namely the multimedia applications. The increasing ability of smartphones and other mobile devices has made these applications one of the major responsible for generating a large volume of data in the contemporary Internet. The authors use the term multimedia sensing as a service (MSaaS) to denote the provision, as a service, of multimedia data from such devices in order to generate information for a variety of applications such as environmental monitoring, monitoring of vital signs of patients, weather forecasting, among others. Another important use of this information is to share content on social networks and online games. Handling the heavy traffic produced by multimedia applications brings great challenges for computer networks, as well as for resource constrained devices resources, particularly regarding energy consumption.

In MSaaS IoT systems, the sensing units basically produce sequences of images or videos, and upload these multimedia streams to servers in the cloud, often via edge/fog nodes. Some users are primarily content producers while other users play interactive cloud video games, in which the traffic intensive multimedia game information is transferred through the wireless access networks [78]. This type of user is primarily a content consumer. Some other types of users are both content producers and consumers. All these users pose severe challenges for MSaaS communications. The authors in the paper focus on the challenges of dealing with the limited battery resources of devices and with the need of guarantying a good quality of experience (QoE) from the consumer side. They propose a new multimedia communication paradigm at application layer, called generalized premium-regular, and investigated new resource allocation strategies to achieve energy efficiency in QoE driven wireless multimedia communications. The context of their work is cloud-edge-fog systems and the focus of their allocation strategies is on the communication resources only, not addressing the other types of resources of an IoT system. They claim that the huge volume of multimedia content must be prioritized to receive the proper treatment and be assigned the necessary resources in the system. The applied their proposed concept of generalized premium-regular to create such differentiate priorities. Traffic classified as premium will be assigned more resources than regular traffic. They thus apply an energy-efficient resource allocation method to deliver the prioritized traffic to the cloud.

Once the pattern of premium-regular based data prioritization at the higher layer is established, cross-layer design at the lower layers is conducted as a complex communication resource allocation problem. They considered several types of communication resources, from the different layers (physical and link) of a networks protocol, and developed a unified premium-based resource allocation methodology to achieve optimal multimedia transmission quality while guaranteeing wireless communication energy efficiency. They formulated the problem as an energy-constrained quality optimization problem, and applied a truncation-point-optimized methodology to solve it. Given a certain communication energy budget, the proposed solution optimizes multimedia quality, by adjusting communication resource parameters such as power and modulation unequally between crucial information (classified as premium) and non-critical information (classified as regular traffic).

5.5.2 Discussion

Recently, some endpoint devices, such as intelligent sensors and actuators and smart handheld devices, have been endowed with significant computing, networking and storage capabilities [79]. As previously discussed, exploring the resources of these devices is valuable in the context of complex IoT systems. However, endpoint devices usually suffer from space, power, bandwidth and security constraints. More robust devices are necessary whenever there is a demand for larger storage resources or for more sophisticated processing of data generated by the interconnected things. In addition, in systems that integrate IoT and cloud, it is necessary to perform some kind of filtering in the data that will be offloaded to the cloud. Injudiciously sending all data collected by devices to the cloud is neither efficient nor desirable from the resource usage point of view. Depending on the application requirements, including the required type of processing and the adopted communication model, the data may not be necessary at all times. Either because the application requests data that are related to a given time interval, or because an intermittent/infrequent event is being tracked, a condition may occur indicating that it is not necessary to transfer the sensed data. In such a scenario, either the sensing device must receive a command to stop producing data or the produced data should not be uploaded to the cloud, in order to avoid wasting resources of the network, the cloud and the devices. Therefore, there is a decision-making component to control this process. Gateway nodes, situated at the edge of the network, in the data path between the data sources and remote cloud data centres, are ideal candidates for playing this role. Besides filtering the data to be sent to the cloud, these nodes may themselves carry out data processing more quickly (in terms of the response time for users) than the cloud and exploiting locality features.

WSN and IoT applications have typically assumed the presence of one or more gateway nodes to perform various functions, but mostly acting as a communication bridge between the different networks. By accumulating more and more responsibilities, in particular by incorporating some decision-making process, such nodes came to be called Smart Gateways, since they became part of the system intelligence. In addition to filtering the data and reconstructing it into a more useful form, uploading only necessary data to the cloud, Smart Gateways can monitor IoT devices and sensors' activities, keeping check on energy consumption of these devices, besides performing data security, privacy, and other generic management functions [73].

Regarding the communication pattern between IoT devices and the Smart Gateway, we observed in the analysed studies that it can be either single-hop or multi-hop. In the first type, sensor nodes and *things* are directly connected to the gateway, which then gathers data from the various devices and sends it to upper layers such as the cloud. This communication model typically applies to small scale systems, where sensing nodes are not so numerous neither heterogeneous and have restricted roles/functions [73]. Examples are IoT systems for smart health applications, where a small number of sensors can be directly connected to the gateway. In such pattern, the communication generally occurs based on a fast monitoring-and-response model. However, when multiple WSN and IoT devices are linked together to achieve more complex goals, direct connection to the gateway is not always possible or efficient. In this case, sub-sets of IoT devices, as well as individual WSNs would have their own sink nodes and/or base stations. The gateway collects the data from those base stations and sink nodes, creating a multi-hop communication scenario. In such scenario, the devices are often more heterogeneous and widely spread, also producing heterogeneous data that requires further processing and extensive data analysis. The gateway would be required to handle heterogeneity regarding the connected devices and collected data, thus dealing with translations and interoperability issues [73]. This kind of scenario is suitable for mobile objects and large-scale IoT/WSN systems, for example, for smart roads, smart buildings and environmental monitoring applications.

Besides the need of dealing with heterogeneity issues, gateways have been tasked with growing requirements of providing context awareness and optimization of system resources, and to offer low latency services for several application domains. These new tasks also brought out the need for collaboration among gateways. Over time, interconnected Smart Gateways evolved to compose a whole new intermediate layer of networking and processing. This new layer is fully aligned with the emergent paradigm of edge or fog computing. The edge/fog tier is usually composed of 'micro' data centres, which in the same way as cloud data centres are strongly based on virtualization but, differently from them, are less powerful and placed closer to the end user.

The proposals discussed in Sect. 5.5 adopted architecture with such an intermediate tier, displaying different degrees of sophistication and capabilities. Table 5.4 summarizes the discussed challenges in IoT scheduling and the studies adopting an edge-based approach that tackled them. We can observe that, differently from the IoT Cloud and IoT only approaches, all proposals that include an edge tier tackle real-time requirements. This corroborates the fact that the edge-based architecture facilitates the building of solutions addressing real-time needs of IoT applications. Another interesting result is the fact that all proposals also provides mechanisms for data stream processing, which is one of the most distinctive features of IoT systems that are often neglected by IoT cloud and IoT

Table 5.4 Comparison of the edge approaches and the IoT challenges they tackled

IoT requirements		Papers		
		[73]	[74]	[78]
High scale		✓	✓	✓
Heterogeneity	Devices	✓	✓	✓
	Applications			
Data stream processing		✓	✓	✓
Dynamic environment			✓	
Opportunistic interactions				
Complex QoS requirements			✓	✓
Context/location-awareness		✓	✓	
Mobility				✓
Fault tolerance			✓	
Application priority				✓
Load balance/fairness				
Real time		✓	✓	✓

only approaches. Regarding the capability of managing the IoT dynamic the environment, proposes such as [74] presents a solution for this requirement that is well-grounded on autonomic principles and self-adaptive systems, allowing the building of truly autonomous and highly scalable resource management solutions for IoT. Finally, we can observe that heterogeneity and high scale are key issues, tackled by all retrieved studies analysed in this section. Fault tolerance, mobility and load balance were the less discussed aspects on these studies.

It is also important to notice that in several proposals the resource monitoring activity was a first-class entity in the system, integrated as part of a control processes based on feedback loops to provide inputs for allocation decisions in an explicit way, ruled by predefined policies.

References

1. Jennings B, Stadler R (2015) Resource management in clouds: survey and research challenges. J Netw Syst Manage 23(3):567–619
2. Nguyen HM, Kim SH, Le DT, Heo S, Im J, Kim D, Optimizations for RFID-based IoT applications on the Cloud. In: 2015 5th international conference on the IEEE Internet of Things (IoT), pp 80–87
3. Dinh HT, Lee C, Niyato D, Wang P (2013) A survey of mobile cloud computing: architecture, applications, and approaches. Wirel Commun Mobile Comput 13(18):1587–1611
4. Yu R, Ding J, Maharjan S, Gjessing S, Zhang Y, Tsang D (2015) Decentralized and optimal resource cooperation in geo-distributed mobile cloud computing. IEEE T Emerg Top Comput 1–1. doi:10.1109/tetc.2015.2479093
5. Xing T, Huang D, Ata S, Medhi D, MobiCloud: a geo-distributed mobile cloud computing platform. In: Proceedings of the 8th international conference on network and service management. International federation for information processing, pp 164–168

6. Baset SA, Wang L, Tang C (2012) Towards an understanding of oversubscription in cloud. In: Presented as part of the 2nd USENIX workshop on hot topics in management of internet, cloud, and enterprise networks and services

7. Caglar F, Gokhale A, iOverbook: managing cloud-based soft real-time applications in a resource-overbooked data center. In: The 7th IEEE international conference on cloud computing (Cloud'14). IEEE, Anchorage, p 10

8. Moreno IS, Xu J (2012) Neural network-based overallocation for improved energy-efficiency in real-time cloud environments. In: 2012 IEEE 15th international symposium on object/component/service-oriented real-time distributed computing. IEEE, pp 119–126

9. Tomás L, Tordsson J (2014) An autonomic approach to risk-aware data center overbooking. IEEE Trans on Cloud Comput 2(3):292–305

10. Caglar F, Shekhar S, Gokhale A, Koutsoukos X, Intelligent, performance interference-aware resource management for IoT Cloud backends. In: 2016 IEEE first international conference on Internet-of-Things Design and Implementation (IoTDI). IEEE, pp 95–105

11. Koh Y, Knauerhase R, Brett P, Bowman M, Wen Z, Pu C (2007) An analysis of performance interference effects in virtual environments. In: 2007 IEEE international symposium on performance analysis of systems and software. IEEE, pp 200–209

12. Hwang J, Zeng S, y Wu F, Wood T (2013) A component-based performance comparison of four hypervisors. In: 2013 IFIP/IEEE international symposium on Integrated Network Management (IM 2013). IEEE, pp 269–276

13. Narman HS, Hossain MS, Atiquzzaman M et al. (2017) Ann Telecommun 72:79. doi:10.1007/s12243-016-0527-6

14. Botta A, de Donato W, Persico V, Pescapé A (2016) Integration of cloud computing and Internet of Things: a survey. Future Gener Comput Syst 56:684–700

15. Renner T, Kliem A, Kao O, The device cloud-applying cloud computing concepts to the Internet of Things. In: Ubiquitous intelligence and computing, 2014 IEEE 11th international conference on and IEEE 11th international conference on and autonomic and trusted computing, and IEEE 14th international conference on scalable computing and communications and its associated workshops (UTC-ATC-ScalCom). IEEE, pp 396–401

16. Kliem A, Kao O (2015) The Internet of Things resource management challenge. In: 2015 IEEE International Conference on Data Science and Data Intensive Systems. IEEE, pp 483–490

17. Kliem A, Boelke A, Grohnert A, Sharing as a principle for medical device management. In: 2015 17th international conference on e-health networking, application & services (HealthCom). IEEE, pp 75–80

18. Yoon Y, Ban D, Han S, An D, Heo E (2016) Device/cloud collaboration framework for intelligence applications. In: Dastjerdi AV, Buyya R (eds) Internet of Things: principles and paradigms. Amsterdam, Elsevier

19. Cox DR (1958) The regression analysis of binary sequences. J Royal Stat Soc Ser B (Methodol) 20:215–242

20. de Santos FJN, Villalonga SG (2015) Exploiting local clouds in the internet of everything environment. In: 2015 23rd Euromicro international conference on parallel, distributed, and network-based processing. IEEE, pp 296–300

21. Rej R (2003) NIST/SEMATECH e-Handbook of statistical methods. Clin Chem 49(6):1033–1034

22. Yu R, Zhang Y, Gjessing S, Xia W, Yang K (2013) Toward cloud-based vehicular networks with efficient resource management. IEEE Netw 27(5):48–55

23. Zanella A, Bui N, Castellani A, Vangelista L, Zorzi M (2014) Internet of Things for smart cities. IEEE Internet of Things J 1(1):22–32

24. Al-Sultan S, Al-Doori MM, Al-Bayatti AH, Zedan H (2014) A comprehensive survey on vehicular Ad Hoc network. J Netw Comput Appl 37:380–392

25. Chang C, Srirama SN, Mass J (2015) A middleware for discovering proximity-based service-oriented industrial Internet of Things. In: 2015 IEEE International Conference on Services Computing (SCC). IEEE, pp 130–137

26. Haghighi PD, Krishnaswamy S, Zaslavsky A, Gaber MM (2008) Reasoning about context in uncertain pervasive computing environments. In: European Conference on Smart Sensing and Context. Springer, pp 112–125

27. Kim J, Lee J-W (2014) OpenIoT: an open service framework for the Internet of Things. In: 2014 IEEE World Forum on Internet of Things (WF-IoT). IEEE, pp 89–93

28. Kefalakis N, Soldatos J, Anagnostopoulos A, Dimitropoulos P (2015) A visual paradigm for IoT solutions development. In: Interoperability and open-source solutions for the Internet of Things. Springer, pp 26–45

29. Martin M, Unbehauen J, Auer S (2010) Improving the performance of semantic web applications with SPARQL query caching. In: Extended Semantic Web Conference, 2010. Springer, pp 304–318

30. El-Mougy A, Ibnkahla M, Hegazy L (2015) Software-defined wireless network architectures for the Internet-of-Things. In: 2015 IEEE 40th Local Computer Networks Conference Workshops (LCN Workshops). IEEE, pp 804–811

31. Ding J, Yu R, Zhang Y, Gjessing S, Tsang DH (2015) Service provider competition and cooperation in cloud-based software defined wireless networks. IEEE Commun Mag 53(11):134–140

32. Giacobbe M, Celesti A, Fazio M, Villari M, Puliafito A (2015) A sustainable energy-aware resource management strategy for IoT Cloud federation. In: 2015 IEEE International Symposium on Systems Engineering (ISSE). IEEE, pp 170–175

33. Dua R, Raja AR, Kakadia D (2014) Virtualization vs containerization to support PaaS. In: 2014 IEEE International Conference on Cloud Engineering (IC2E). IEEE, pp 610–614

34. Akyildiz IF, Su W, Sankarasubramaniam Y, Cayirci E (2002) Wireless sensor networks: a survey. Comput Netw 38(4):393–422

35. Li J, Qiu M, Niu J-W, Chen T (2011) Battery-aware task scheduling in distributed mobile systems with lifetime constraint. In: 16th Asia and South Pacific Design Automation Conference (ASP-DAC 2011). IEEE, pp 743–748

36. Pathak A, Prasanna VK (2010) Energy-efficient task mapping for data-driven sensor network macroprogramming. IEEE Trans Comput 59(7):955–968

37. Li W, Delicato FC, Zomaya AY (2013) Adaptive energy-efficient scheduling for hierarchical wireless sensor networks. ACM Trans on Sens Netw (TOSN) 9(3):33

38. Gutierrez-Garcia JO, Sim KM (2013) A family of heuristics for agent-based elastic cloud bag-of-tasks concurrent scheduling. Future Gener Comput Syst 29(7):1682–1699

39. Gen M, Lin L (2014) Multiobjective evolutionary algorithm for manufacturing scheduling problems: state-of-the-art survey. J Intell Manuf 25(5):849–866

40. Caliskanelli I, Harbin J, Indrusiak LS, Mitchell P, Chesmore D, Polack F (2012) Runtime optimisation in WSNs for load balancing using pheromone signalling. In: 2012 IEEE 3rd international conference on Networked Embedded Systems for Every Application (NESEA). IEEE, pp 1–8

41. Delgado C, Gállego JR, Canales M, Ortín J, Bousnina S, Cesana M (2016) On optimal resource allocation in virtual sensor networks. Ad Hoc Network

42. Li W, Wang S, Cui Y, Cheng X, Xin R, Al-Rodhaan MA, Al-Dhelaan A (2014) AP association for proportional fairness in multirate WLANs. IEEE/ACM Trans Networking 22(1):191–202

43. Shi Y, Hou YT, Liu J, Kompella S (2013) Bridging the gap between protocol and physical models for wireless networks. IEEE Trans Mob Comput 12(7):1404–1416

44. Sharief M, Kingston O, Hossam S, Kingston O (2012) Resource re-use in wireless sensor networks: Realizing a synergetic internet of things. J Commun 7(7):484–493

45. Oteafy SM, Hassanein HS (2012) Towards a global IoT: resource re-utilization in WSNs. In: 2012 international conference on computing, networking and communications (ICNC). IEEE, pp 617–622

46. Li W, Delicato FC, Pires PF, Lee YC, Zomaya AY, Miceli C, Pirmez L (2014) Efficient allocation of resources in multiple heterogeneous wireless sensor networks. J Parallel Distrib Comput 74(1):1775–1788

47. Delicato FC, Portocarrero JM, Silva JR, Pires PF, de Araújo RP, Batista T (2013) MARINE: MiddlewAre for resource and mIssion-oriented sensor NEtworks. ACM SIGMOBILE Mobile Comput Commun Rev 17(1):40–54

48. Li L, Li S, Zhao S (2014) QoS-aware scheduling of services-oriented internet of things. IEEE Trans Industr Inf 10(2):1497–1505

49. Almeida L, Fischmeister S, Anand M, Lee I (2007) A dynamic scheduling approach to designing flexible safety-critical systems. In: Proceedings of the 7th ACM & IEEE international conference on Embedded software. ACM, pp 67–74

50. Agirre A, Parra J, Armentia A, Ghoneim A, Estévez E, Marcos M (2015) QoS management for dependable sensory environments. Multimedia Tools Appl 1–23

51. Agirre A, Parra J, Armentia A, Estévez E, Marcos M (2016) QoS Aware middleware support for dynamically reconfigurable component based IoT applications. Int J Distrib Sens Netw 12(4). Article ID 2702789, p 17. doi:10.1155/2016/2702789

52. Joseph M, Pandya P (1986) Finding response times in a real-time system. Comput J 29(5):390–395

53. Takalo-Mattila J, Kiljander J, Pramudianto F, Ferrera E (2014) Architecture for mixed criticality resource management in Internet of Things. In: TRON Symposium (TRONSHOW). IEEE, pp 1–9

54. Viswanathan H, Lee EK, Pompili D (2012) Mobile grid computing for data-and patient-centric ubiquitous healthcare. In: 2012 First IEEE workshop on Enabling Technologies for Smartphone and Internet of Things (ETSIoT). IEEE, pp 36–41

55. Kim M, Ko I-Y (2015) An efficient resource allocation approach based on a genetic algorithm for composite services in IoT environments. In: 2015 IEEE International Conference on Web Services (ICWS). IEEE, pp 543–550

56. Zhu Q, Wang R, Chen Q, Liu Y, Qin W (2010) Iot gateway: bridgingwireless sensor networks into Internet of Things. In: 2010 IEEE/IFIP 8th international conference on Embedded and Ubiquitous Computing (EUC). IEEE, pp 347–352

57. Vögler M, Schleicher J, Inzinger C, Nastic S, Sehic S, Dustdar S (2015) LEONORE–large-scale provisioning of resource-constrained IoT deployments. In: 2015 IEEE Symposium on Service-Oriented System Engineering (SOSE). IEEE, pp 78–87

58. Billet B, Issarny V (2014) From task graphs to concrete actions: a new task mapping algorithm for the future Internet of Things. In: 2014 IEEE 11th international conference on mobile Ad Hoc and sensor systems. IEEE, pp 470–478

59. Jünger M, Liebling TM, Naddef D, Nemhauser GL, Pulleyblank WR, Reinelt G, Rinaldi G, Wolsey LA (2009) 50 years of integer programming 1958–2008: from the early years to the state-of-the-art. Springer Science & Business Media

60. Angelakis V, Avgouleas I, Pappas N, Fitzgerald E, Yuan D (2015) Allocation of heterogeneous resources of an IoT Device to flexible services. IEEE Internet Things J 3(5):691–700. ISSN: 2327–4662

61. Colistra G, Pilloni V, Atzori L (2014) The problem of task allocation in the Internet of Things and the consensus-based approach. Comput Netw 73:98–111

62. Schenato L, Gamba G (2007) A distributed consensus protocol for clock synchronization in wireless sensor network. In: 46th IEEE conference on decision and control. IEEE, pp 2289–2294

63. Kliem A, Renner T (2015) Towards on-demand resource provisioning for IoT environments. In: Asian conference on intelligent information and database systems. Springer, pp 484–493

64. Farias CMD, Li W, Delicato FC, Pirmez L, Zomaya AY, Pires PF, Souza JND (2016) A systematic review of shared sensor networks. ACM Comput Surv (CSUR) 48(4):51

65. Teixeira T, Hachem S, Issarny V, Georgantas N (2011) Service oriented middleware for the Internet of Things: a perspective. In: European conference on a service-based internet. Springer, Berlin, pp 220–229

66. Garcia Lopez P, Montresor A, Epema D, Datta A, Higashino T, Iamnitchi A, Barcellos M, Felber P, Riviere E (2015) Edge-centric computing: vision and challenges. ACM SIGCOMM Comput Commun Rev 45(5):37–42

67. Hu YC, Patel M, Sabella D, Sprecher N, Young V (2015) Mobile edge computing—a key technology towards 5G. ETSI White Paper 11
68. Bonomi F, Milito R, Zhu J, Addepalli S (2012) Fog computing and its role in the Internet of Things. In: Proceedings of the first edition of the MCC workshop on Mobile cloud computing. ACM, pp 13–16
69. Verbelen T, Simoens P, De Turck F, Dhoedt B (2012) Cloudlets: bringing the cloud to the mobile user. In: Proceedings of the third ACM workshop on mobile cloud computing and services. ACM, pp 29–36
70. Pahl C, Lee B (2015) Containers and clusters for edge cloud architectures–a technology review. In: 3rd International Conference on IEEE, Future Internet of Things and Cloud (FiCloud), pp 379–386
71. Al-Fuqaha A, Guizani M, Mohammadi M, Aledhari M, Ayyash M (2015) Internet of things: a survey on enabling technologies, protocols, and applications. IEEE Commun Surv Tutorials 17(4):2347–2376
72. Armbrust M, Fox A, Griffith R, Joseph AD, Katz RH, Konwinski A, Lee G, Patterson DA, Rabkin A, Stoica I (2009) Above the clouds: a berkeley view of cloud computing. Tech Rep UCB/EECS-2009-28, EECS Department, University of California, Berkeley, Feb 2009
73. Aazam M, Huh E-N (2014) Fog computing and smart gateway based communication for cloud of things. In: International Conference on IEEE, Future Internet of Things and Cloud (FiCloud), pp 464–470
74. Cardellini V, Grassi V, Lo Presti F, Nardelli M (2015) Distributed QoS-aware scheduling in storm. In: Proceedings of the 9th ACM international conference on distributed event-based systems. ACM, pp 344–347
75. Marz N (2014) Apache storm. Git repository [online] https://git-wip-us.apache.org/repos/asf
76. Pietzuch P, Ledlie J, Shneidman J, Roussopoulos M, Welsh M, Seltzer M (2006) Network-aware operator placement for stream-processing systems. In: 22nd International Conference on Data Engineering (ICDE'06). IEEE, pp 49–49
77. Kephart JO, Chess DM (2003) The vision of autonomic computing. Computer 36(1):41–50
78. Wang W, Wang Q, Sohraby K (2016) Multimedia Sensing as a Service (MSaaS): Exploring resource saving potentials of at Cloud-edge IoTs and fogs. IEEE Internet of Things J 99:1–1. doi:10.1109/JIOT.2016.2578722
79. Byers CC, Wetterwald P (2015) Fog computing distributing data and intelligence for resiliency and scale necessary for IoT: the Internet Of Things (ubiquity symposium). Ubiquity 4

Chapter 6
Concluding Remarks and Open Issues

Abstract The emergent paradigm of Internet of Things (IoT) has the potential to provide novel value-added services to increase the quality of life of citizens, increase the productivity of companies and promote building more intelligent and sustainable cities, environments and countries. Despite its potential benefits, there are still many challenges to be overcome to leverage the wide dissemination and adoption of the IoT paradigm. One major challenge in this context is *efficiently managing the resources involved in an IoT ecosystem*. In this Book, we presented the state of the art in the area of resource management for IoT, with focus on characterizing the architectures and infrastructures able to support all the activities involved in such process. This chapter presents our final remarks, including a summarization regarding the activities addressed by the works discussed throughout the Book and the open issues identified. There are still several research opportunities to be explored in the field of resource management in order to tackle all the challenges posed by the IoT ecosystems in this context.

Keywords Internet of Things (IoT) · Cloud of things · Wireless sensor networks · Resource management · Resource allocation · Resource discovery · Resource modelling

6.1 Final Remarks

We carried out a systematic literature review to acquire the inputs for the discussions and analysis presented along this book. The works retrieved as outcome of such literature review propose different architectural approaches, techniques and models for all the key activities considered as part of a resource management system (RMS) for IoT. As we mentioned in Chap. 2, we identified the following activities as the main components of a typical workflow for an IoT RMS: resource modelling, resource discovery, resource estimation, resource allocation and resource monitoring. Considering such key activities, we found that the resource estimation was the activity that appears less in the analyzed studies, followed by the

F.C. Delicato et al., *Resource Management for Internet of Things*,
SpringerBriefs in Computer Science, DOI 10.1007/978-3-319-54247-8_6

resource discovery. We believe this was expected, since this activity is not crucial for the proper operation of an RMS, but it only contributes to potentially increase its efficiency and the satisfaction of the users. By estimating a priori, the resources required to execute an application, both the over and under provisioning can be avoided. But the ad hoc and dynamic features of IoT ecosystems surely pose a challenge to accurately estimate resources. Surprisingly, the resource discovery activity was often neglected as part of a holistic RMS and addressed mostly in the context of service-oriented middleware approaches. Actually, the authors in [1] claim that current IoT architectures still lack support for an efficient and standard way for discovering services, followed by their composition and integration in a scalable way. Lack of effective strategies for service/resource discovery can result in execution delays, poor user experience and runtime failures [2].

The resource allocation activity is the most extensively investigated so far. It is important to mention that works focused only on algorithmic optimization procedures for resource allocation in IoT are out of the scope of this book. However, for the sake of completeness, we present below a brief discussion on algorithm solutions for IoT RM so that the interested reader can seek for more detailed information on the pointed references.

Most works addressing the resource allocation and scheduling in IoT employ an approach based on multi-objective optimization problems (MOOP). MOOP extends the traditional single objective optimization to take into consideration optimization decisions involving more than one objective function to be optimized simultaneously. Multi-objective optimization has been applied in solving problems where optimal decisions need to be taken in the presence of trade-offs between two or more conflicting objectives and are generally proposed to present a set of solutions, which are optimal in the sense that none of them are better than the other if all the objectives are considered. In this case, the objective functions are said to be conflicting, and there exists a possibly infinite number of solutions. A solution is called Pareto optimal or Pareto efficient if none of the objective functions can be improved in value without degrading some of the other objective values. The goal of any MOOP algorithm is to effectively and efficiently achieve a Pareto-optimal set [3]. In the field of IoT resource allocation and scheduling, MOOP is commonly applied to minimize the resource usage while maximizing system lifetime or resource fairness having as constraints the application QoS requirements. For instance, in [4], the authors proposed a solution to maximize the system lifetime under the constrains of data accuracy and energy consumption.

One important feature to be considered when applying MOOP in the IoT domain is that such problems are generally NP-hard to solve. Therefore, to find out the optimal solution on time, in such large and complex system, is non-trivial. Multiple techniques can be found in the literature to address this issue. Heuristic and metaheuristic approaches have been applied by many works [4–11] due to its simplicity and low response time even when providing near-optimal solutions. Other solutions found in the literature are linear programming [12] and ε-approximation [13].

6.2   Open Issues

Most studies reported in the current literature and discussed throughout this book meet, either fully or partially, one or more requirements that we consider relevant for an IoT RMS. The tables presented in Chap. 5 depict the discussed works in the light of these requirements. Figure 6.1 summarizes such tables showing how many works address each one of the IoT requirements.

As we can observe from Fig. 6.1, there are still some open issues, i.e. requirements that have not been extensively analyzed, which we will discuss below.

Data stream processing and real-time processing. Data stream processing is a key functionality of IoT systems and the discussed proposals still lack from fully tackling the challenges of properly allocating resources for such type of processing. Several authors discuss the need of providing online solutions to accommodate the data stream oriented features of IoT. We also discussed proposals that modelled the dynamic characteristic of resource consumption as a requirement for allocating resources for data streams. However, some specific requirements, such as combining online and offline communication and processing, transaction management operations [14], among others, were not considered in the presented proposals. Moreover, there are several tasks involved in a typical workflow for data stream processing, such as (i) pre-processing, (ii) dimensionality reduction, (iii) feature extraction and (iv) abstraction inference. Such tasks demand resources from the IoT system and the proper allocation of them to each of the 2 or 3 tiers is crucial to promote the system efficiency. For instance, by allocating a pre-processing task to the Things tier, it is possible to reduce a lot the usage of the communication

Fig. 6.1 IoT requirements addressed by the discussed works

resources. There is a challenging resource allocation problem regarding the proper assignment of data stream processing tasks, which is still lacking from proper solutions. Regarding the real-time processing, we noticed that such requirement was only considered in solutions designed for a specific application domain. For instance, eHealth is typically a time critical application, and therefore resource allocation solutions for such domain must consider real-time processing. Moreover, the emergence of edge computing as part of the IoT architecture was strongly motivating for this requirement, so most proposals addressing real time come from this field.

Application Priority. Although most resource allocation solutions take into account the application QoS requirements in their decision-making, there are still solutions that consider only the functional requirements to build their application model. There is still no consensus on the relevant QoS requirements for IoT, and some solutions use only typical network requirements. More complex requirements, specific for IoT application domains, are still not satisfactorily addressed by existing solutions. In addition, we observed a big gap with respect to works considering different priorities between applications. This may be because the existing proposals, either are completely agnostic to the application domain or are used in a specific domain. The coexistence of multiple applications, from various domains, with different requirements and criticality levels is a subject still little explored.

Opportunistic interactions. Finally, as we observed in the Fig. 6.1, one of the requirements less exploited by the resource management proposals is dealing with opportunistic interactions that emerge in the IoT ecosystem. This type of interaction has been highly exploited in the field of participatory sensing (PS). PS is an interesting and novel approach that aims to leverage the capacities of sensing available mainly in devices as smartphones, and utilizes them as active sensory platforms for monitoring their immediate environment. By intelligently combining these individual sensor readings, it is possible to create a picture of the physical world at unprecedented spatiotemporal granularity, to be used as input to various IoT applications [15]. As described in [15], there are several steps involved in building a typical PS application. These steps include, after collecting the sensed data, transferring them to a remote data centre (often at the cloud) for long-term storage and processing. Existing proposals typically assume the existence of a manual configuration process where users will choose different policies for this data transfer, regarding the type of network to be used (i.e. cellular, WiFi, Bluetooth). After the transfer, there is a step for storing and managing such data in the data centre. These steps certainly involve decisions of resource management that are not being addressed in the PS literature so far. Decisions on the transfer and storage of data can be fully automated by an RMS to increase the effectiveness and efficiency of the system. Because our study is focused on the IoT field, no discussed work except [16] was from the PS area. Moreover, we notice in the existing work a lack of convergence between the areas of IoT and PS, although it is easy to see PS as a subset of IoT. We believe that the full potential of IoT will be achieved only when this kind of opportunity use of volatile resources available temporarily in the environment is exploited effectively, bringing benefits to all types of users.

A Comprehensive Pricing Model for IoT. Another issue relevant to our analysis, and that is indirectly related to resource management activities, refers to the pricing model for IoT. This issue was addressed only in few retrieved works and always in the context of cloud or fog. When IoT resources are provided as a service, it is natural to inherit the model used in cloud computing, where contracts are established (SLA) and prices are paid according to the amount of resources used, the time duration of the usage and the delivered quality of service. Proposals in which the IoT resources are virtualized and provided as a service can adopt a pricing model where the users pay for the use of these virtual resources in the same way they would pay for the use of cores and virtual machines in traditional data centres. However, there are new factors that must be considered when charging for services generated from IoT devices. For example, in order to keep the freshness of the virtual representation of sensing data (maintained by the cloud or fog tier), the resources of the physical device need to be frequently accessed, thus consuming the device hardware and battery. Therefore, one must include in the pricing model the cost of using these physical resources along with the virtual ones. We did not find in the retrieved works pricing models explicitly including this type of cost. Moreover, just as in P2P networks, end users can participate in an IoT ecosystem both as consumers and as service providers. We have seen in our survey that there are works that stimulate the active participation of the device owners via collaboration as a way of decreasing the price to be paid for the use of the IoT infrastructure. But in general, such works only use simple approaches where collaboration is encouraged for the purpose of decreasing the total price paid. There are no complex models that take full advantage of the capabilities of IoT devices and effectively calculate a monetary cost for the use of these resources. We also saw that in SDN approaches, prices may be assigned to software-defined IoT units, thus allowing charging IoT resources as utilities. However again, in the retrieved works there is no specific proposal for a novel pricing model explicitly computing cost of using IoT devices.

In this context, one of the few works that actually proposes an innovative pricing model for IoT is described in [16]. The authors propose a framework for priced public sensing (PPS) in smart cities based on an IoT architectural model that integrates heterogeneous data sources. Their proposal was developed in the context of an emergent paradigm that is closed related to IoT, called Public (or Participatory) Sensing (PS). Put simply, participatory sensing is the concept whereby individuals, groups and communities use the increasing capabilities of mobile phones and other personal devices, along with cloud services, to collect and analyze sensing data in order to compose a body of knowledge for use in several applications. The idea is to leverage the participation of citizens as providers of different types of sensory data and at the same time empower them with knowledge about critical issues related to security, pollution, traffic conditions and other aspects of the daily life in urban societies. Large-scale WSNs, IoT and data stream processing systems are the underpinning of such paradigm [17]. In [16], the authors tackle the challenges of providing a comprehensive public sensing model, encompassing policies for incentive data sharing in order to motivate device owners to participate in the sensing process and to ensure that the provided data is fairly priced. They consider a multi-tier PPS framework with four main components. At the top tier of their proposed architecture, Access Points (APs), owned by service providers, initiate data requests based on queries issued by clients. Sensing data is at the lower tier of the architecture which includes Light Nodes (LNs) comprising sensors, smart devices, RFID tags and other IoT devices. Each group of LNs is assumed to form a peripheral network according to their deployment and application specifications. Their framework adopts the approach in which the LNs are passive entities, exclusively dedicated to data collection. Each LN delivers its sensed data by multi-hop transmission through other LNs to one or more Data Collectors (DC). Data collectors are equipped with wireless transceivers or RFID readers and are responsible for forwarding the LNs' data load to gateways (GWs). Gateways are more sophisticated devices which are connected to the cloud via the Internet or any other backhaul. Furthermore, GWs perform an intermediary role by replying to AP data requests in addition to providing them with pricing parameters. Sensed data provided by the PPS framework is delivered upon client's request in exchange for a monetary charge or a price to be compensated for by the requesting party. The data is priced according to attributes related to the LN's resource availability such as energy, transmission capacity and the collective lifetime of the peripheral network it belongs to. This latter attribute is decided by the GW connecting the peripheral network to the cloud, which simultaneously acts as an intermediary on behalf of LNs. The requesting party, on the other hand, is to decide on the suitability of the price according to a utility function that considers the user's service requirements. To accommodate these different needs, the authors provide a two-tier dynamic pricing scheme [16]. At the lower tier, GWs reply to AP data requests with a resource-based service price. At the top tier, the requesting AP generates a utility function based on the user's service requirements, his/her affordable price limit and on the available GW replies to choose from. Their model also differentiates between the users' requirements in terms of delay and quality of the delivered data, categorizing the data in different types according to such requirements. Although this proposal is the most comprehensive in terms of inclusion of the cost of using the device resources for calculating the price of an IoT service, still the only type of service provided by such devices is sensing. They do not consider that the processing resources, although limited, can also be explored and priced.

We claim that the resource management activities need to be revisited in view of the specific requirements of IoT. We believe that a truly top-down vision for the design of a resource management system for IoT is required where such requirements guide all its design. As the IoT area is still very new, existing solutions are still immature. In the works found and analyzed throughout this book, a dominating trend is the adaptation of cloud or wireless sensor networks solutions to the new domain of IoT. We believe that there is still a gap regarding the holistic solutions to manage IoT resources throughout their life cycle, from its representation at design time to their efficient allocation and monitoring at run time. The interconnection of the several players from different layers/tiers/tiers, the division of the workload between them in a fair and efficient way, and the inclusion of actuation operations as part of the required tasks, are challenges that we believe remain to be fully tackled. Moreover, we believe that to support the expected ultra large scale of the IoT along with its dynamic and opportunist characteristics, it is a key requirement that the resource management system is endowed with self-management features. Systems able to monitor the execution environment, learning from past and current behaviour, self-adapting, Self-healing and self-optimises according to the context with minimal external intervention are the most promising solution to tackle all the IoT challenges and intelligently orchestrating the available resources.

Acknowledgements   We would like to express our sincere gratitude to Jorge Pereira da Silva and Porfirio Gomes, from the Federal University of Rio Grande do Norte, Brazil, and to Dr. Wei Li, from the University of Sydney, Australia. Their valuable help by performing the literature review and the initial compilation and summarization of the relevant works was crucial to the writing of this Book. Flavia Delicato and Paulo Pires would like to express their deep gratitude to Professor Albert Y. Zomaya, from the University of Sydney, for hosting us along the year of 2016, during which we developed part of this work. This work was partially supported by Brazilian Funding Agencies FAPERJ (under grant number 213967 for Flavia C. Delicato) and CNPq (under grants numbers 200757/2015-6 and 307378/2014-4 for Flavia C. Delicato, 310958/2015-6, 457783/2014, and 200758/2015-2 for Paulo F. Pires. For Thais Batista, this work was partially supported by the Brazilian National Agency of Petroleum, Natural Gas and Biofuels through the PRH-22/ANP/MCTI Program and by CNPq under grant 308725/2013-1. Flavia C. Delicato, Paulo F. Pires and Thais Batista are CNPq fellows.

References

1. Wei Q, Jin Z (2012) Service discovery for internet of things: a context-awareness perspective. In: Proceedings of the fourth Asia-Pacific symposium on internetware. ACM, p 25
2. Buyya R, Dastjerdi AV (2016) Internet of Things: principles and paradigms. Elsevier, Amsterdam
3. Chakraborti S, Sanyal S (2015) An elitist simulated annealing algorithm for solving multi objective optimization problems in Internet of Things design. Int J Adv Netw Appl 7(3):2784
4. Li W, Delicato FC, Pires PF, Lee YC, Zomaya AY, Miceli C, Pirmez L (2014) Efficient allocation of resources in multiple heterogeneous wireless sensor networks. J Parallel Distrib Comput 74(1):1775–1788
5. Choi Y, Lim Y (2016) Optimization approach for resource allocation on cloud computing for IoT. Int J Distrib Sens Netw. 2016(23)
6. Colistra G, Pilloni V, Atzori L (2014) The problem of task allocation in the internet of things and the consensus-based approach. Comput Netw 73:98–111
7. Giacobbe M, Celesti A, Fazio M, Villari M, Puliafito A (2015) A sustainable energy-aware resource management strategy for IoT Cloud federation. In: 2015 IEEE International Symposium on Systems Engineering (ISSE). IEEE, pp 170–175
8. Hassani A, Haghighi PD, Jayaraman PP (2015) Context-aware recruitment scheme for opportunistic mobile crowdsensing. In: 2015 IEEE 21st International Conference on Parallel and Distributed Systems (ICPADS). IEEE, pp 266–273
9. Liu T-C, Wang K, Ku C-Y, Hsu Y-H (2016) QoS-aware resource management for multimedia traffic report systems over LTE-A. Comput Netw 94:375–389

10. Maior HA, Rao S (2014) A self-governing, decentralized, extensible Internet of Things to share electrical power efficiently. In: 2014 IEEE International Conference on Automation Science and Engineering (CASE), 2014. IEEE, pp 37–43
11. Billet B, Issarny V (2014) From task graphs to concrete actions: a new task mapping algorithm for the future internet of things. In: 2014 IEEE 11th international conference on mobile Ad Hoc and sensor systems. IEEE, pp 470–478
12. Angelakis V, Avgouleas I, Pappas N, Fitzgerald E, Yuan D (2015) Allocation of heterogeneous resources of an IoT device to flexible services. IEEE Internet of Things J 3 (5):691–700
13. Tahir Y, Yang S, Adeel U, McCann J (2015) Symbiot: congestion-driven multi-resource fairness for multi-user sensor networks. In: 2015 IEEE 17th international conference on High Performance Computing and Communications (HPCC), 2015 IEEE 7th international symposium on Cyberspace Safety and Security (CSS), 2015 IEEE 12th International Conferen on Embedded Software and Systems (ICESS). IEEE, pp 654–659
14. Abu-Elkheir M, Hayajneh M, Ali NA (2013) Data management for the internet of things: design primitives and solution. Sensors 13(11):15582–15612
15. Tilak S (2013) Real-world deployments of participatory sensing applications: current trends and future directions. ISRN Sensors Netw 2013(583165) , p 8. doi:10.1155/2013/583165
16. Al-Fagih AE, Al-Turjman FM, Alsalih WM, Hassanein HS (2013) A priced public sensing framework for heterogeneous IoT architectures. IEEE Trans Emerg Topics Comput 1(1): 133–147
17. Estrin D, Chandy KM, Young RM, Smarr L, Odlyzko A, Clark D, Reding V, Ishida T, Sharma S, Cerf VG (2010) Participatory sensing: applications and architecture [internet predictions]. IEEE Internet Comput 14(1):12–42

Index

© The Author(s) 2017
F.C. Delicato et al., *Resource Management for Internet of Things*,
SpringerBriefs in Computer Science, DOI 10.1007/978-3-319-54247-8